IRONDRESSES

Strength in Femininity

IRONDRESSES

Strength in Femininity

Cherelle Z. Johnson

IRONDRESSES
Strength in Femininity

Unless otherwise identified, Scripture quotations are from the New Living Translation. Copyright © 1996, 2004, 2015 by Tyndale House Foundation. Used by permission of Tyndale House Publishers, Inc., Carol Stream, Illinois 60188. All rights reserved.

Scripture quotations marked (NIV) are taken from the Holy Bible, New International Version®, NIV®. Copyright © 1973, 1978, 1984, 2011 by Biblica, Inc.™ Used by permission of Zondervan. All rights reserved worldwide. www.zondervan.com

Final Step Publishing, LLC

PO Box 1441
Suffolk, VA 23439

For Worldwide Distribution. Printed in U.S.A.

Soft cover ISBN: 978-1-4903252-8-6

DEDICATION

This book is dedicated to the woman who is searching. She is on the brink of truth and needs that extra push of encouragement to live her dream. She is full of potential but is just one dress size, grade, degree, or promotion away from her normal. This is to the woman who is wearing so many hats she forgets which one she was born with.

Regardless of your past, lack of resources, or excessive ridicule, I dare you to be a women identified by strength, identified by God.

CONTENTS

ACKNOWLEDGMENTS

Thank you, Lord for ordering my steps with your grace and mercy.

Karrin Jones & Refine Graphics, LLC. Thank you so much for your graphic design work and your encouragement to complete this project! Big thanks to *Dr. Kerrita Mayfield* for volunteering her sketches.

Angel Mosley and Rebecca Wineland. Thank you for your dedication to critique and edit this book! Your service to me means more than you'll ever know! *Dr. Joanne Gabbin*, thank you for all your wisdom and encouragement.

IronDresses Team. You ladies are the ingredients needed for the vision for IronDresses Inc. to move forward. Thank you for your dedication, support, and friendship.

DUCC Family. Thank you for allowing me to be a revived woman, active to glorify God. I am reminded to live in vision every time I am in your midst. I will forever be Called-Connected-Committed.

Chris Johnson. Thank you for being the man you are: a man of integrity, transparency, and passion. Your desire to see my dreams come true is amazing. Thank you for being my best friend-husband. You look good on that cross. You are my romance.

FOREWORD

"In a loud voice she exclaimed:
'Blessed are you among women...'"
Luke 1:42

I n 1956, the deodorant *Secret* hit the stage. Secret's aim was to provide women the protection they need to take on life fearlessly—"to live arms up." Within a few years of this female brand deodorant, one of the most popular ad slogans emerged saying, "Secret is strong enough for a man, but made for a woman." This slogan captured the mission of the deodorant because it celebrated and liberated women to be women. Not less than, not like a man, but to be a woman.

We are at a critical time in our society to differentiate between what it means to be equal and what it means to be the same. Our culture is slowly eroding at the seams of sexuality and gender. Equal does not mean the "same." There are differences in men and women which need to be highlighted, celebrated, and encouraged. When a man is being 100 percent what he is supposed to be, it encourages the woman to be 100 percent what she needs to be and vice versa.

When Cherelle began to recognize this, a great burden arose in her to empower women to celebrate the strength in their femininity. *IronDresses* celebrates and encourages women to be unapologetically themselves. This book identifies four aspects of women and encourages them to strive to be the best mother, sister, daughter, and wife they can be. This book bridges generational gaps, heals open wounds from weakened and torn identities, and draws you closer to living out what God has so graciously invested in you. I am convinced and confident that God uniquely designed women to be women and men to be men; therefore, in order for us to please our Creator, we must identify and celebrate these wonderful distinctions. It is my prayer that as you read this, you will be challenged and encouraged to "live arms up" surrendered to Christ, taking life on fearlessly by embracing your strength in your femininity. After reading *IronDresses,* I can truly say that like the *Secret* deodorant, this is "Strong enough for a man, but made for a woman."

Chris Johnson
Lead Pastor
Divine Unity Community Church
Harrisonburg, VA
www.ducchurch.org

INTRODUCTION

IronDresses started as my collection of thoughts about the things I have learned and continue to learn about being a Christian woman! Little did I know that what I assumed were just thoughts would birth vision to my passion for empowering women. *IronDresses* is a reflection of my passions and gifts displayed through educating women and restoring communities. Honestly, I had no desire to write a book. This is just my organizational way of sharing my journey with Christ to a community of women. But as you can see, God intervened with my plans, so this is indeed a book.

IronDresses is more than my book title … it is my heart's cry and framework for womanhood. *IronDresses* is a movement with a goal to restore and empower women of all ages to live in the strength of their femininity. It is all about exploring and celebrating our strength that is housed in our femininity. That's right ladies, as we explore who God created us to be, we will find that being a woman is not a *side note* to our identity. Being a woman is the main event! We are identified by God and characterized by the strength in our femininity

Why the name *IronDresses*? Iron is a solid metal chemical element that is everywhere! It is the most common element in the whole planet. It's used to build the world around us, as well as keep plants and animals alive. The chemical symbol for Iron is *Fe*. I think it's cute that the symbol for iron is *Fe*, the same English letters that separate the sexes: male and *fe*male. *Iron* represents strength, and *dresses* denotes femininity.

Fashion is a large part of cultures around the world, and I believe that a dress is a type of clothing that screams femininity. Simply because a person had a vision for a style, it goes on the runway and is considered haute couture. I would love for the Word of God to govern the lives of women in such a way that when it is exposed on this runway of life, we give our all to make sure we are fashionably dressed for the season … the season that God has created for us.

Proverbs 27:17 states, "As iron sharpens iron, so one person sharpens another." This scripture emphasizes the sharpening or improvement that is created only when elements of the same makeup connect. We are warrior princesses, so let's get to work and support one another in our journey through womanhood. Being led by the Holy Spirit, let's check each other's wardrobe, formerly known as your lifestyle. During this check, you may need to assist with some spring cleaning or organizing. This may be the season for you to borrow a dress or two. There may be some dresses that will never be worn again, so chuck them! Or you may need to just iron some things before making a final decision.

Chapter 1

feminine Infirmity

*W*hat is your infirmity? Do you ever see your femininity as a weakness? Do you ever find yourself competing with others around you? Do you ever feel like you do not measure up to those around you? Do you view your womanhood as something that is crippling? Well, let me inspire you to be free. Be free to celebrate your femininity.

Luke 13:10-13 states,

"On a Sabbath Jesus was teaching in one of the synagogues, and a woman was there who had been crippled by a spirit for eighteen years. She was bent over and could not straighten up at all. When Jesus saw her, he called her forward and said to her, 'Woman, you are set free from your infirmity.' Then he put his hands on her, and immediately she straightened up and praised God."

"Woman, you are set free from your infirmity." Jesus is so aware of His authority that He *reached* out to this woman in her infirmity and strengthened her. In other words, Jesus said, "You are released, you are healed, you are loosed, and you are set free!" I would imagine that Jesus was amped. I mean, He was doing what He was destined to do … setting the captives free. And here is another example of His doing so prior to the resurrection.

If you want to know anything about me, know I am excited that He said "woman" in this passage. There are many instances in scripture where it states he, him, man, men. Sometimes it translates to men only; other times it's universal. The only argument that comes to mind when the Bible states "woman" would be if the text was speaking to a married or unmarried female and its tone. In this text, there is no debate as to whom Jesus was speaking. "Woman," He called, and never even mentioned her bondage.

He called her forward. Jesus saw her and called her forward. He called her after Him. In order to be healed, set free, and delivered, you must MOVE! Your movement should be in response to following the voice or inspiration of God. Sometimes we have to visit our pasts in order to learn, let go, unlock blame, and forgive. Even though our pasts seem to take us backward, reflection is vital for our progression. Many times, we remain in the bondage of our infirmity because we are not willing to move at all. I read a great book by Erwin McManus called *Chasing Daylight,* and it is all about moving forward. It talks about how God has already given the "go," and it takes action on our part. Usually, that action is our faith.

When Jesus saw her, He called her. I wonder if there was a time-lapse between the time Jesus saw and called her and when He laid His hands on her and immediately, she was strengthened. Again, she received what she needed because she recognized He was talking to her. It is so important to grow in relationship with the Lord, so we recognize His communication with us. Samuel was young and did not know that the Lord was calling his name, but thanks to his mentor Eli, he was then prepared to receive a word from the Lord (1 Samuel 3:9). Be a sister by saying, "Hey Sasha, God is calling you." Don't allow your sister to be crippled by the lies of this world. Don't let jealously hinder your ministry of womanhood. Take some time to embrace her, so she can straighten up and praise the Lord.

"On a Sabbath Jesus was teaching in one of the synagogues, and a woman was there who had been crippled by a spirit for eighteen years" (vs 13). I love it. On the day of rest, this woman was at church, at Bible study, listening to Jesus, Himself, teach. It is great being in the right place at the right time, attempting to learn. She was crippled by an evil spirit for eighteen years! Can you see this? Think about graduating from high school conditioned to live a life of bondage. Think of how crippling that would be; yet because it had been a way of life, you were no longer sensitive to the pain. You did not see it. The scripture did not mention she was in pain. She didn't even ask to be healed, but Jesus saw her.

In Robert Kegan's research about Transformative Learning (1982), he argues that in life, you have the ability and should strive to move from being *subject to object.* Now, as far as I know, he was not making a biblical statement at all, but I completely interpreted that theory through biblical understanding. Moving from *subject to object* is a theory that explores the difference of things having you versus you having things. Concepts having you, versus you having concepts. What do I mean by this? Things or situations in your life that are *subject* to you are experiences that you do not question because it is a part of you. Really, you cannot *see* these emotions, assumptions, or behaviors because they are a part of you. It has you. These could be blind spots or strongholds due to a developed belief system. When situations move to *object,* you become introduced to alternatives or options. You can reflect on it. You have it. The more situations you take as an *object,* the more complex you become because you have more options to act on while things that are *subject* are unknown and unnamed. Things that are *object* are revealed, have reflection, and responsibility.

The "garment of praise" is the antidote to the spirit of heaviness.

It is interesting that the woman in this scripture had an eighteen-year sickness that caused her physical body to submit to the disease. Are you being controlled by an evil spirit that refused you the ability to have a better perspective? My husband has done a lot of studying on evil spirits. The spirit of heaviness is what brings forth burdens and emotions that drain our energy. The spirit of heaviness rests on us to make it difficult for us to praise God. This is where such things as anxiety and depression come from. The "garment of praise" is the antidote to the spirit of heaviness (Isaiah 61:3 KJV). Ultimately, as a believer in Jesus Christ, that spirit should not define or confine you. You do not have to carry that baggage. The enemy has an infirmity that you are not subject to. As you arrive at that truth, you can reflect and take responsibility for your life. You *are* subject to the imprint of Christ that is knitted into your spiritual DNA. This truth will set you free.

I think I get so excited when reading this passage because I just see myself. We should call this lady "Cherelle." I can see it so clearly. I was nineteen years old, sitting on a dorm couch at Bridgewater College. I was in the presence of the teaching of Jesus Christ and had no idea I was crippled. I guess I was just at the right place at the right time because from that day forth, I believe Jesus called me forward and healed my spiritual infirmity. My spiritual metabolism had a boost. My soul began to long for Christ, the truth, like never before. God allowed my sin to be an *object* in my life. As He revealed the bitterness, fear, insecurities, and pride, I was no longer subject to a sinful posture, much like the woman in the scripture who was bent over and could not straighten up.

What keeps you bent over? What's heavy on you? Christ says that His yoke is easy and His burden is light (Matt. 11:30). What are you looking at on the floor? What's the posture of your heart? Simply reading your Bible over and over may cause you to appear straight and in right standing. You may be able to quote scripture, comprehend the message, and even teach others, but if you are simply relying on your religious habits to maintain your posture, you are still living with the infirmity. Do you dress modestly in order to be recognized as that, or is it the posture of your heart? Are you driven to live righteously so your gossip is justified, or do you hunger and thirst for righteousness? Are you being a servant in church under Mr. Man of God in order to display your qualities as a wife, or are you embracing your singleness as a gift of service to the church? This can be a scary thing to witness. The lady was crippled in the place of healing, yet subjected to her lifestyle. Can you identify with this lady?

My desire is for women to live freely, not in bondage. Our identity as women doesn't have to be subject to our infirmities. Genesis 3:16 says, "Unto the woman he said, I will greatly multiply thy sorrow and thy conception; in sorrow thou shalt bring forth children; and thy desire shall be to thy husband, and he shall rule over thee" (KJV). I believe that this does not only mean that giving birth will feel like flirting with death, but also suggests that your *concept* of self will be in greater distress. Your identity and that of your husband›s will be tainted. A woman became a pioneer into sin, but a woman also gave birth to salvation (1 Tim. 2:15).

It's because of our faith in Christ that we are no longer slaves to sin. John 3:16 states, "For God so loved the world, that He gave His only begotten Son, that whosoever believeth in Him should not perish, but have everlasting life." I challenge your feminine self to live according to that new covenant of truth yet manage the knowledge of the fall of mankind. You have the option to live in Christ and not perish with regret. You have the option to possess an eternal, non-transitory life. and not grieve your design. You are a mother pregnant with the conception of self. Make a life-affirming decision to be the WOMAN, set free of her infirmity. This is the essence of IronDresses!

> My desire is for women to live freely, not in bondage. Our identity as women doesn't have to be subject to our infirmities.

5

In Reflection:

Take time to re-read Luke 13:10-13.

1. In the text, Jesus called a woman forward after she had dealt with an issue for eighteen years. Recall a time when you struggled with something for a long time. Did the Lord call you forward? If so, did you recognize it as Him and did you take action? If not, why?

2. Taking action requires faith. What are you struggling with that requires stepping out in faith? Are you ready to give it to God?

3. Being clothed in a garment of praise is the anecdote for a spirit of heaviness. When praising God with your arms surrendered, you can't hold on to anything. What is it you need to let go of so you can praise God?

4. Letting go of something often requires giving up something you may have been holding on to for quite some time such as a bad habit or relationship. Are you ready to release whatever it is you've been holding on to so God can heal you?

5. Set aside some time to pray. Ask God for the courage to step forward in faith and to let go of what's been holding you back. If you need support, contact someone who can help hold you accountable.

Chapter 2

Be Lovely

*B*eauty is such a complex paradigm with several elements and perspectives. We crave beauty. It provides harbor where we can rest in peace. Beauty instigates protest and debate. God created beauty as a pasture for a woman's soul. In 1 Peter 3:4, we are reminded that true beauty is holy! She is inward and incorruptible and very precious in the sight of God. Beauty is an essence of womanhood that needs not to be robbed. She offers pleasure to the senses and mind. Many times, we deprive beauty by making her the equivalent to perfection.

Bible teacher and author Beth Moore stated that "perfectionism is an insecurity in its art form." Do you remember the geometry rule that states a square is a rectangle, but a rectangle is not a square? Well, I would say that perfection is beautiful, but beauty is not perfection. Beauty shapes more like a quadrilateral (a two-dimensional shape with four sides, with interior angles that add up to three-hundred sixty degrees). Quadrilaterals have core principles in common, but they have much diversity to display. Parallelograms, rectangles, rhombuses, squares, trapezoids, and kites are all quadrilaterals that serve different purposes with different corner angles. The variety of beauty displays purpose and poise and anchors the complete three-hundred sixty degrees of womanhood.

In all that mess, God creates beauty. He crafted beauty from beauty because only the woman houses a womb.

Not only did God know us before we were formed, but Psalms 139:13-14 reminds us that God created our inmost beings and knitted us together in the wombs of our mothers. He created us to be full of reverence and wonder. Have you ever thought about what the inside of a womb looks like? To this day, my husband still cringes from the memory of seeing the placenta delivered after our daughter's birth. The womb may not be the most pleasant picture, yet God does His pure work in that place. Oh, the irony of beauty! In all that mess, God creates beauty. He crafted beauty from beauty because only the woman houses a womb. How special is that? Women are beauty's greenhouse: the home where beauty starts as an inward seed and with care grows to become distributable to others. That's been the goal since your conception—to see the beauty cultivated in this world in order to give honor to the gardener who created us. Although He created us beautiful, the only way we will truly display it is when we surrender it to Him. In order to keep beauty holy, we must exchange our thoughts about beauty in return for a paradigm shift.

> In order to keep beauty holy, we must exchange our thoughts about beauty in return for a paradigm shift.

Be Lovely in Form and Feature

> *"This girl, who was also known as*
> *Esther, was lovely in form and feature..."*
> Esther 2:7 (NIV)

To be lovely in form and feature is to understand and believe that you were created for such a time as this. This understanding will allow you to know that your biblical beauty will set others free as you unveil your worth. Loveliness suggests something charming and agreeable. Being lovely is a benefit. Scriptures describe Esther as lovely, and it was to her benefit that this attribute was noticed. Loveliness is a silhouette of beauty that appeals to the heart, as well as the eye. When you address someone as lovely, you are not just saying they are cute, pretty, or solely nice looking. You are acknowledging the beauty inward and out.

Your *form* is your body. Yes, ladies, Esther›s body had it going on too. The scripture did not describe her physical appearance beyond addressing that it was lovely. Sometimes, we can deprive beauty by elevating our warped opinions of our bodies instead of the truth. When you look at yourself, do you refer to your body as lovely? If not, is this due to unconfessed sin or the core belief of lies? Have you ever complained about your weight but continued to eat unhealthily? Have you ever felt self-conscience about your shape, but continued to wear that low-cut, high-cut dress? Have you ever cringed while looking at a blemish or physical deformity, yet continued to accept non-covenanted sexuality? Have you ever called yourself ugly but failed to contemplate God's infinite purpose for how you look?

If so, I believe that this is a result of a warped view of our forms. You are not a horrible person if you do not like your physical body, but there may be a negative seed planted that is contrary to the Word of God. Psalm 139:14 says that we are fearfully and wonderfully made. Our bodies are so valuable that they are the place where the Holy Spirit dwells and are referred to as "temples" (1 Cor. 6:19). Do you look at your church building and have negative thoughts about its appearance? The construction workers would not appreciate that. This is one of the reasons Romans 12:1 urges us to submit our bodies to the Lord and to be transformed by renewing our minds. If not, the view of our bodies could lead to a destructive and manipulated place that was never in the blueprint for our purposes.

Your *feature* is your distinctive mark by the Lord. These are your characteristics that serve as His fragrance to this world. The writer of 2 Corinthians 2:15 declares that "we are the sweet fragrance of Christ" to the saved and unsaved.

> Our bodies are so valuable that they are the place where the Holy Spirit dwells and are referred to as "temples."

Our features represent how we were fashioned. Jeremiah 1:5 tells us that we were sanctified and ordained before we even had a form. How awesome is this! Have you ever asked yourself these questions: What is God trying to tell my nation or generation through me? What is my specific scent?

We were created on, in, and with purpose. This is the mystical part of our beauty that can be overshadowed by other aspects of life. Esther's parents died, leaving her as an orphan. She was raised by her male cousin. She did not have documented female influence in her life and was an exiled Jew. There could have been many excuses for Esther if she had not been lovely, but her circumstances did not win. Her features were so strong that it really could not have been explained in any other way. Esther pleased the king, and she received favor! This favor then promoted her from being an orphaned girl to an outstanding queen. With this authority, she surrendered confidence in her own ability (Esther 4:11-17) and received the courage to save her people from destruction.

Lovely Confidence

Lovely confidence is surrendered confidence. It is an agreeable strength for a lady. Confidence is very visible. On the days where I am not feeling confident, I miss out on the beauty. I find faults in others and I am extra picky in a way that is not edifying. On my good days, I trust completely in the Lord, which puts my confidence on a high. This has nothing to do with anything outward; this is a result of that inner truth by which God formed me. To be confident is to have full trust in the Lord. True confidence is great attire. It is contagious and encouraging for others while being merely conceited is a benefit to no one. When confidence in natural abilities are surrendered, (through prayer and fasting or a pure hunger for God), the fragrance of Christ in us is overwhelming. Proverbs 3:5 says "Trust in the Lord with all your heart, And lean not on your own understanding." Have you ever been in a situation where you were confident in yourself and not Christ? How did that turn out? Have you ever avoided a situation because of your lack of confidence? What could you learn from that situation?

When you have the confidence that you are lovely in form and feature, you are in the position to set some things free. Renewing your mind and feasting on the truth about who you are will posture your life to receive favor from the King! With this favor, He will put you in the best places and around the best people with a specific task in mind. Understanding that you are lovely will reference true humility and attain authority. With this authority, you see yourself as a vessel for the Lord to set the captives free. You view yourself as an ambassador for Christ, knowing that God is pleading through your life. Indeed, being lovely in form and feature presents heavy responsibility, but the best part is that you were created for such a time as this from the beginning.

So, when you are in a bad mood and feeling some-type-of-way about yourself, be sure to enhance your beauty treatments. These treatments consist of spiritual disciplines such as prayer and fasting, meditation, giving, and studying the Word of God. The treatment does not make you beautiful. Its purpose is to polish in order to uncover your original shine. We were born into sin and shaped into iniquity, but through the work of Christ on the cross and our acceptance, we are made new again. We are polished and buffed for our original beauty to illuminate.

In Reflection:

1. Before you began this study, how did you define beauty? Now that you've read a few chapters, what does beauty mean to you?

2. In the text, beauty is described as providing harbor and rest. How do you think that can be so?

3. Beauty is not the equivalent of perfection. How do you think something or someone can have beauty and flaws at the same time? Do you think something can be perfect yet not have beauty? Explain your answer.

4. We talk about being lovely in form and feature. What are some biblical principles that support this idea? (I encourage you to look up scripture for this one.)

5. Part of being lovely is having lovely confidence or surrendered confidence. What does this look like to you?

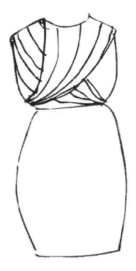

Chapter 3
Iron Affairs

*M*y good friend Angel has an idea of romance captured in a scene from the story collection, *Anne of Green Gables*. It's some sweet, loving scene where Gilbert professes his love for Anne, even after she rejects his marriage proposals. Poor Anne realizes her true feelings for her childhood friend, Gilbert, years later, after learning he is engaged to another mutual friend. Her heart is broken until she learns that he called off the engagement for her sake, explaining, "There will never be anyone for me but you ..." As you can guess, they later lived happily ever after. I have never seen the movie version (even after a few sneak attempts by Angel at my most vulnerable moments), but I could picture the couple holding hands and frolicking down the dirt path into the sunset.

On the other hand, my idea of a romantic scene is the ending of the movie *Mr. and Mrs. Smith*. Yes, the scene when they are in the warehouse shooting their enemies back to back! *[Sigh]* how lovely. Lead is flying everywhere at a deadly speed. I love it! These two "romantic" scenes are extremely different, yet they have a unique similarity: the truth revealed always conquers!

One day while exercising, Angel and I had a great conversation about her favorite scripture: 2 Tim. 2:2-4. Unknowingly, after that conversation, my outlook of my journey as a Christian shifted. The term *affair* has many meanings. One can refer to a political, romantic, family, or private affair. An affair is simply a special function or personal event. For this purpose, an Iron Affair is a special and personal event with Christ. Just like a romantic scene, there are many different interpretations of the meaning of strength. In the scheme of *IronDresses*, iron represents the strength found in our identities as females. This is only true because we were created female by God.

Strength in the Promise

Strength is not contingent on what you have, but what has you. In 2 Corinthians 12:9, the author explains that in our weaknesses the Lord's strength is perfected, therefore, we can confess our weaknesses without shame. The promise of God positions us to be covered by His perfection. God gives us grace for our weaknesses. This grace is so powerful that it completely overshadows the weakness. Paul pleaded for his thorn to be removed, but God told him that what He had was sufficient because of grace. Our testimony will continually be that Jesus did it, not me.

With this in mind, you have to be tutored for the proper affairs. It is declared in 2 Timothy 2:4 that "No one serving as a soldier gets entangled in civilian affairs, but rather tries to please his commanding officer" (NIV).

The commander is the Lord! Yes, you are a warrior princess! You are an ambassador for Christ, as though God were pleading through you. God has already implored you to **The Bible is all about Christ and serves as our guide to be ambassadors for Him.** be reconciled and serve others in harmony with the Father. Civilian affairs are matters and situations that belong to the individuals who are not Christian. If one has not accepted Christ as their Lord and Savior, they are subject as civilians, natives of this world (instead of heaven-bound). The sad reality is that we were never created to be merely civilians, and those who believe the opposite may be forfeiting their position in everlasting life.

Ladies let's open our pretty eyes. There is plenty of corruption in this world, and it is vital that we stay armed with the Word of God. This is the best weapon because it is infallible and full of promises. The Bible is all about Christ and serves as our guide to be ambassadors for Him. With the many attacks set out for women in our society, it's so vital to know the promises of God for your life. Traps such as sex trafficking, eating disorders, abuse, and abortion somehow seem to flood the lady market and distort our view of our true strength. This seems to be what happens when we are not aware of God's promise.

What happens when distorted obedience causes distress? Sarah's maidservant Hagar knew all about this. Genesis 16 refers to the story about Hagar. She was an Egyptian which probably meant she did not believe in the true God. Hagar was able to bare children, unlike Sarah at the time; therefore, she was used as a substitute to give birth to Abraham's child. The harsh reality is that Hagar may have truly been unaware of God's promise for Abraham. In their custom, it was not uncommon for men to sleep with servants to have children, so Hagar was just doing her job. When we do not know the promises of God, we may settle for substitutes. In many instances, this can look like you are just doing your job or doing what you are told. A female civilian is vicariously taught to just live accordingly. The standard weight for a woman is *this* and height is *that*. Body exposure is what attracts. Exclusive sex is safe sex. These accepted standards are contrary to God's full promises for us.

Have you ever felt like you were in this pit, a place where you feel stuck? Beth Moore taught about three ways one can get into a pit. She explained that you can be thrown into a pit, you can slip into a pit, or you can put yourself in a pit. Uncontrollable sin around you can throw you in a pit, but you must choose to get out. Something good gone bad can be your catalyst for slipping into a pit, but you must exercise moderation and not addiction. Finally, when you willfully choose sin, you are putting yourself in a pit. With all this being said, Beth Moore's bottom line was to encourage the listener to get out of the pit. Hebrews 12:1 instructs us to "lay aside every weight, and the sin which so easily ensnares us, and let us run with endurance the race that is set before us." How is this possible in the world we live in today? This scripture continues by telling us to fix our eyes or focus on Jesus who perfects our faith. When we fix our eyes on Jesus, we are looking at God's

The exclusive and innate ability to be a mother, daughter, sister, or wife is a huge aspect of your identity.

promise. This is the true seed He promised to Abraham. When we believe the promise that God will never leave us or forsake us, we are relying on His strength within us to persevere. David realized this as he walked through the pit in the valley of the shadow of death. He did not fear because he knew the promise that God was with him.

The mere truth that God created you as a woman in his image should sober your thoughts. Being a woman is not secondary; it is how you specifically identify with your Christian affairs! The exclusive and innate ability to be a mother, daughter, sister, or wife is a huge aspect of your identity. It seems like Hagar got entangled in civilian affairs and was thrown into a pit.

It is one thing to notice and have a desire to make a difference for civilians' sake, but it's another thing when you subject yourself to a lifestyle that doesn't breed truth from your design. Women are powerful! And God created strength in your femininity. Any time you disregard the fact that you are a woman, you sacrifice part of your strength. Refuse to ignore your feminine identity when considering God's promises. Living in the affairs of Christ mandates an abundant life in response to His promises. Do not just settle for existing; live abundantly in response. You dwell in God's abundant grace and mercy. You exude in His abundant beauty. You shelter His abundant peace. Dignity is a state of nobility. It is a token of respect, significance, and distinction. Acting with dignity elevates your rank. In other words, ladies, rock your royalty! We are heirs of the King! Know your inheritance, because that will reveal your identity and strength.

In 1 Peter 2: 9-10 it states,

"But you are a chosen generation, a royal priesthood, a holy nation, His own special people, that you may proclaim the praises of Him who called you out of darkness into His marvelous light; who once were not a people but are now the people of God, who had not obtained mercy but now have obtained mercy."

Iron Armor

As warrior princesses, we must always wear our armor, as instructed in Ephesians 6:14-18. Paul wrote this letter while he was captured by Roman soldiers, and this uniform was inspired by his guards. Because the fight is not against flesh and blood, we must wear spiritual uniforms for battle. With the proper attire, we will be clothed in strength and dignity. Our armor equips us with truth, righteousness, peace, faith, and salvation.

"Stand therefore, having girded your waist with truth" (vs. 14). Stand up straight (with your hands near your waist, hip somewhat leaned toward the right, left leg slightly bent, right calf flexed) and protect your figure with that belt of truth! Never leave the house without it. This truth is what holds everything together. Forsaking your belt of truth will cause the armor to be faulty. This protection-truth always sets you free to be active.

"... having put on the breastplate of righteousness" (vs. 14b). Ladies, the proper bra for your body type will maintain your righteousness! Just kidding ... maybe. Well, think about it. Your breasts are the second most physical feminine aspect of your being. It's second to your hot spot, better known as your vagina. What is the purpose of a bra? For protection, right? You did not create or produce your own natural breasts; they were inherited. Your breasts were assigned to you according to your DNA. It's the same with righteousness, being in right standing with God. You cannot work for righteousness; you can only work to guard (to show acceptance toward) what was given to you by God. We alone are not worthy of anything apart from Christ. He did the work, and we live in response to that. Putting on the breastplate of righteousness is purposely protecting your vital organs of righteousness.

"... and having shod your feet with the preparation of the gospel of peace" (vs. 15). Getting a pedicure is great maintenance, but wearing the proper shoes for your season will put you in a ready position. No matter how common the rest of your outfit looks, appropriate shoes will always be a game-changer. In the same way, the Gospel is your foundation and will always prepare you for your next move. The Gospel presents you with insight to the type of terrain you will be treading, and it is essential to your mobility.

"... above all, taking the shield of faith with which you will be able to quench all the fiery darts of the wicked one. And take the helmet of salvation and the sword of the Spirit, which is the word of God" (vs. 17). The weather can be unpredictable; and in some cases, you must proceed regardless. It is vital to shield yourself with faith, salvation, and the Word because you are constantly *wearing* your truth, righteousness, and proper footwear. This umbrella of faith, which covers the entire body, will not only stop the conditions from harming you, it will also quench its power of attack. It›s one thing to have a dart thrown at you, but a dart on fire. This fire has a mission to destroy, not just harm. We know that the wicked one is only present to kill, steal, and destroy. Keeping your shield of faith is a reminder that Christ came to give life and life more abundantly. Taking your headgear gives extra strength to protect from discouragement. As you are being transformed by the renewing of your mind, you should take caution in protecting your mind.

Finally, the Word of God is your offense weapon. Hebrews 4:12 states, "For the word of God is quick, and powerful, and sharper than any two-edged sword, piercing even to the dividing asunder of soul and spirit, and of the joints and marrow, and is a discerner of the thoughts and intents of the heart." Ladies, as warriors, it is not enough to show up in our armor; we must use it! We must apply what is true to our daily lives and this takes practice.

"… praying always with all prayer and supplication in the Spirit, being watchful to this end with all perseverance and supplication for all the saints" (vs 18). This is the final touch to our armor as well as our marching orders. There is no way to please our commanding officer without direct communication with Him! Prayer is how we enter the battle. And don't forget, a warrior princess is in battle not only for herself but also for the safety of others.

Wearing this armor, I believe that I am more beautiful now than ever in life. It is not because I've lost weight. It is not because my hair is healthier and longer, or that I age gracefully, but because I strive to allow Christ to adorn me. I am not a civilian, I am a Christian. It's war time, ladies, and I hope you are encouraged to pick up your iron and sharpen it in preparation for battle. Don't forget, we are warrior princesses; so, we fight together and in dresses! (War cry) AHHH! Live free from your infirmities, in abundance, and in the affairs of Christ.

In Reflection:

1. We gain strength in holding onto God's promises. What promises from God are especially meaningful to you?

2. Describe a time when you held onto a promise from God in spite of the waiting period? How did things work out?

3. Reflect on a time when you tried intervening in a situation instead of waiting on God to fulfill a promise. How did things turn out in this situation?

4. Oftentimes we have trouble seeing ourselves as warrior princesses because of our sinful natures. God's promises can reaffirm our royalty. What are some scriptures that reinforce your heritage in the kingdom of God? If you don't know of any, take time to look them up. Pray and ask God to direct you.

5. To be effective as a princess warrior, you must be clothed with your spiritual armor, which requires daily use or otherwise it becomes rusty and ineffective. Take time to assess your armor and determine how battle-ready you are. What areas do you need work on?

Chapter 4
Worship Wardrobe

$\mathcal{O}$ ne lovely day, my husband and I were in the mall doing a little shopping, and we came across a men's clothing store. It didn't have many clothing options, but regardless, my husband was drawn directly to the three-piece suits. As we were chatting with the salesman, my eyes ran across a line of preaching robes. I joked (*what I thought was a joke*) with Chris seeing if he wanted to purchase one. At this time, we were a couple of months away from our official church launch date, where Chris would serve as lead pastor of Divine Unity Community Church (DUCC). Although DUCC is a non-denominational church, we were both raised in Baptist churches where the preachers wore robes. I had no idea that wearing a robe could be an option for my husband simply because we have such a non-traditional style of ministry, and quite frankly, I have never seen him preach in a robe. Little did I know that this joke would make room for an intense conversation.

As Chris roamed through the small selections of robes, I chuckled at his attempt to play along ... *or so I thought*. This man was actually considering my suggestion. Now, I am in no way attempting to offend any clergymen who abide by this discipline, but it was simply something I did not imagine him doing. As time went on, Chris did not see a robe he liked, so I had to finally ask him, "Were you seriously considering getting a robe?" I know my facial expression provided much more detail than my words at that time. I am pretty sure the space between my eyebrows came together to make an indention while my left lip slightly tilted upward, really displaying, *Why in the WORLD would you considering getting a robe?* My patient husband simply took the time to explain, to my opinionated self, the biblical significance of the priest wearing a robe during ministry time. He explained that a robe was considered consecrated clothing of the priest and was only used during the ministry moments.

As he continued with this wardrobe lesson, it stirred many of my thoughts about the current attire of women. Why don't I view my clothing as consecrated garments? How would that change my outfit choice as well as my definition of ministry? These thoughts just added yet another reason for me to wear dresses more often. What if a dress was considered consecrated clothing of women in today's context? Could you imagine? Do you think more women would wear dresses? Would modest apparel be a subject for debate still? Take a look into your wardrobe and examine your clothing. Do your clothes distinguish you in a way that puts the attention on Christ? What about the attire of your heart? What is in the closet of your heart? Does that organ bleed the fuel of a consecrated lady? If not, I would encourage you to start building a worship wardrobe full of dresses for edification, education, and equality.

Dresses for Edification (Worship)

1Tim. 2:9-15 states,
"In like manner also, that the women adorn themselves in modest apparel, with propriety and moderation, not with braided hair or gold or pearls or costly clothing, but, which is proper for women professing godliness, with good works. Let a woman learn in silence with all submission. And I do not permit a woman to teach or to have authority over a man, but to be in silence. For Adam was formed first, then Eve. And Adam was not deceived, but the woman being deceived, fell into transgression. Nevertheless she will be saved in childbearing if they continue in faith, love, and holiness, with self-control."

OK, so where do I start? This is a very controversial scripture. I wonder if Paul knew the extent of frustration he would cause for us when he was giving Timothy these instructions on worship. Or is it that we've complicated things over the years? I guess because Paul was in his later years he was not trying to please people at all. He had a mission to set order for Timothy and Titus at that time. Regardless, we do know that Paul cared deeply. He viewed Timothy as his true son. When he began this letter, he gave the clear goal that the command was to love *"from a pure heart, from good conscience, and from sincere faith"* (1Tim. 1:5). Now, I am not a Bible scholar, but I am going to attempt to explain my perception of the above scripture. My purpose is not at all to prove anyone wrong or start a riot, although I like a good debate. The history of women has gone from breastfeeding to burning bras, to the creation of breastfeeding bras. I just want ladies to be informed in the midst of it all.

"In like manner also," Paul instructs men to first honor God in worship, and then he put an equal demand on women. The instructions for the woman's attire are just as important as the instruction for the man's reverence to prayer. *Adorn*, is an action word that means to arrange, prepare, make ready for, or to embellish with honor. *Modesty* is a term that seems to have lost its value. I think it is sad that to some, modest apparel is simply not being nude in public. To dress modestly is to dress in a manner that does not draw attention to yourself. I believe Paul is simply saying to dress appropriately for worship (life) and to not intentionally make your appearance the center of attention with your hairstyle, jewelry, and clothing. Just because you are wearing a long, dark green dress that covers your fingertips, is made to fit two people, and is designed by a company called "Modest Wear," that does not fulfill this scripture. Now, am I encouraging you not to be fly? Not at all.

> To dress modestly is to dress in a manner that does not draw attention to yourself.

I am encouraging you to spend more time conversing with the Lord than you spend getting dressed. If it takes you thirty minutes to pick out an outfit, try to allow God to pour into your life for at least thirty minutes prior. Besides, it is the *IronDress* within you that will be the showstopper anyway.

In Paul's letter to the Romans, he urges us to be transformed by the renewing of our minds. Dresses for edification is not a style I am restricting you to but a mindset I would call forth. Let's love one another by wearing the truth. Instead of telling you what you should not wear, I would rather encourage you to put on love. Colossians 3 reminds us to clothe ourselves with compassion. We are to put on a new self, renewed in the knowledge and the image of God.

Dresses for Education

In 1 Tim. 2:11 it says, "Let a woman learn in silence with all submission." This instruction picks my brain because I am mostly extroverted. This means that I am energized by people and more focused on the outer world. In short, it is helpful for me to speak to think clearly, while others—introverts—think in order to speak. Because of this, my husband asked me to let him know when I am talking to him or just thinking, since he can hear both at times. Paul says, "learn in silence." In assuming that *thinking* is a part of learning, this means for a girl like me, I need to SPEAK. Now, how do I speak silently? This drives me crazy.

When researching the term *silence* in the lexicon, I was enlightened to see that the biblical usage in the text is referring to domestic behavior—the home. Silence or quietness is requesting that the wife remain focused and not to meddle in things that could have negative results. In other words, stop trying to control everything. The first time the first woman, Eve, tried to control matters and put herself above, she welcomed sin into the world!

Submission means to release your personal agenda and accept that of another's. It means to give of yourself or to come under another's mission. When you submit your resume to a job, you do not ask for it back. When you are hired, you do not add your old job responsibilities to this one. You take on a new role (with training from the Holy Spirit HR department). I am not in any way conveying that to be submissive one must become a "doormat." Actually, it takes a secure person of purpose, who has foresight beyond themselves, to choose submission. I think it's hard to be successfully submissive and learn loudly. Try to spend quality time with God while attempting to control Him at the same time. Let's see how that works out.

When I was getting my master's degree, I learned and grew so much. One of my favorite courses was Learning Theories. This class exposed me to many different theories about how adults learn. Conditioning theories suggest that learning is a result of your environment and that mental processes are not necessary to explain behavior change. Well, of course, we are past that theory.

The social cognitive learning theory states that we use our brain to learn (go figure) and emphasizes learning in a social environment. Accordingly, learning occurs by doing, observing, reading, and listening. The constructivist theory suggests that no scientific truth exists; it is discovered. It contends that learners form their own understanding of knowledge and skills. The one thing these theories have in common is the notion that learning is an enduring change in behavior resulting from something. In this scripture, to learn in silence is also to change your behavior, release control of your husband, and give yourself to him. If you are not married, the same applies to you, except your marital submission is to God only. Release control to the Lord and change in behavior with all submission. I wonder if Paul really wanted to say "Ladies, stop complaining, nagging, gossiping, and telling men what to do! Listen to the Lord." And men, *let* her do just that. Yes, surrender yourself in prayer without anger so she can listen *with* you. I'm just wondering if that would be the modern translation.

As women, we do not have to compete with or prove our similarities to a man in order to justify our equality.

Dresses for Equality

As women, we do not have to compete with or prove our similarities to a man in order to justify our equality. Embracing womanhood does all the balancing. Equality is rooted in identity and it takes value to steward fair treatment. Genesis 1:27 states, "God created man in his own image, in the image of God he created him; male and female He created them." Next, God blessed them and gave a corporate mission. God said it was very good, male and female, so why do we try to challenge that worth? Authority does not suggest equality, rather it suggests responsibility. God gave both the woman and man authority. I believe we just have to accept the differences in responsibility.

1 Timothy 2:13-15

"For Adam was formed first, then Eve. And Adam was not deceived, but the woman being deceived, fell into transgression. Nevertheless she will be saved in childbearing if they continue in faith, love, and holiness, with self-control."

1 Corinthians 11:11-12

"Nevertheless, neither is man independent of woman, nor woman independent of man, in the Lord. For as woman came from man, even so man also comes through woman; but all things are from God."

These scriptures are among my favorites on this topic because they are so life-giving. It shows how God's grace is an essence of who He is. *Nevertheless* is such a grace-filled word! It is a word that gives hope to a previously smeared premise. Yes, Eve sinned. She ate the fruit. She took the bait and pioneered a new life for her and Adam. This does not make her less of God's creation. She was not a second-rate person due to her mistake, thanks to grace. I am not sure if God is witty in His sovereignty or not, but I find it funny that Satan endeavored to use the woman to distance humanity, God's very *good* creation. God used the woman to birth the bridge—Jesus—that would reconcile humanity back to Him. I am not keeping a tally here, but you must admit, the Savior of the world entered the world through a girl. There was no male assistance whatsoever in this instance. This has to counteract something, right? The Christian story shows on a large scale, how "all things work together for the good of those who love God and are called according to his purpose" (Romans 8:28).

In today's culture, unexpected pregnancy is looked at as a curse or an inconvenience, when biblically speaking it is a sign of redemption. Being pregnant saves a life rather than ruins a life. This may be a controversial perspective, but I hope that you are able to see the parallel of God's design of redemption through our femininity. This is something that a man will never experience, but that doesn't make him greater than or less than. Our equality comes from embracing the totality of our womanhood. This divine view of femininity is what I hope you can gain. God designed you with all you need to be equal when you are walking according to His design for you.

Addie's Dress

Human Resource Development (HRD) is all about designing structure and performance improvement. During my first semester of graduate school, we learned about the ADDIE model, a key component to HRD at large. ADDIE is an acronym for Analysis, Development, Design, Implement and Evaluate. Although we are learning how to apply this model in the workforce, I could not help but see how this model is a way of life. ADDIE is not just a generic model; she's what Tyra Banks would call "type fierce." Addie is a woman who is confident in her God-given identity. She knows her design as a female and is Christ's diplomat on this earth. Addie is a Proverbs 31 brand woman.

The first thing Addie does is **analyzes** the situation at hand. She analyzes with her spiritual eyes. She takes the time to pray and meditate on God›s Word because she knows it will cut through the junk. This phase is crucial because it unveils the difference between what is actually happening and what should be happening. Addie then **designs** her objectives. She speaks things into existence. She has the faith of a mustard seed without seeing the outcome. In this phase, she considers her target audience and makes the appropriate moves. Next, Addie **develops** her modules. She actively listens, always remembering that God controls the time. Shet hen **implements** her plan. "She sets about her work vigorously; her arms are strong for the task" (Proverbs 31:17). Addie believes that God has created her for such a time as this as well. Her actions affect other women. She is a doer, not just a hearer of the Word. Finally, Addie continually **evaluates** her experiences and exposures. She asks the Lord, «What season is it now?» She invites the presence of God everywhere she is in order to determine the value of her situation.

I pray that you allow the Holy Spirit to develop your worship wardrobe. Make sure you have dresses for worship that are compassionate. This is a dress that is embellished with honor but not self-centered. You need dresses for education that change behavior as a result of the truth. This dress is not controlling, yet it is giving of itself. Lastly, be sure to have dresses for equality. These dresses are distinctively feminine yet have the exact same manufacturer as a man's tie—marked by the same designer but for different purposes. There is so much strength in your femininity! Don't forget to model it!

In Reflection:

1. Take an assessment of your clothing wardrobe. What does it say about you? How does it reflect your feminine nature?

2. Now take an assessment of your spiritual wardrobe. What does it say about you? How does it reflect your feminine nature?

3. When you consider wardrobe basics such as prayer, compassion, and giving, in what areas do you need to expand your spiritual wardrobe?

4. In implementing the Addie Dress method, how can you incorporate accountability into your life to ensure you are properly dressed for worship?

5. One of the keys to having the proper spiritual wardrobe is to be renewed by the transformation of your mind. What areas of your mind need renewal? Pray and ask God to give you strength in doing so.

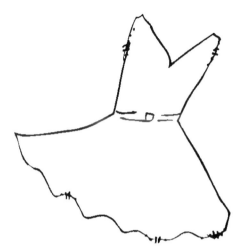

Chapter 5
Dresses-4-Life

*L*uke 12:35 (NIV) states, "Be dressed ready for service and keep your lamps burning." What does this look like? Is it putting on stockings with your fitted purple suit, pumps, and hat, and carrying a lit candle in your purse? I don't know about you, but for me, the Bible can be quite comical, especially when read out of context. According to this scripture, to be dressed and ready for service is to have a posture focused on Christ. More specifically, it is to be focused on His second coming.

The military is a great practical example of being ready for service. My mother was a Marine. She joined when she was twenty and had to attend boot camp, which was basic training for the service. She had to wear a specific uniform, take classes, and pass tests. My mom lived across the country while a Marine. This was her service. She never fought in a war or was part of a risky mission, but while on duty, she was always dressed and ready for service.

Now imagine yourself getting ready for a date with the finest man ever! He is the epitome of who you want to live your life with, and he's going to pick you up sometime after 7 p.m. You'd be ready for his arrival no later than 6:45 p.m. As a matter of fact, you would pick your outfit out days before and have your girlfriends over or ready on the phone to chat until he gets there. Because you are so focused on the one to come, nothing else matters much, not your job or your schoolwork. You even forgot about your ex-boo who did you so wrong. You are ready for the one to come.

Being dressed and ready for service is a dynamic life. Your service is all about preparation. You are preparing for Christ to come again. Having a relationship with truth is what really compels you for service. I read a commentary that put it quite simply. It stated, "You may have an inner willingness to serve God [being dressed], but not have the illumination you need to serve Him well [keeping the lamp burning]." The psalmist expressed in chapter 119 verse 105 that, "Your [God's] word is a lamp for my feet and a light on my path." God's Word is the guide for your life. To be ready for service without the Word of God is like preparing for the wrong date. It is to not be ready at all. Be dressed for service and keep your lamps burning. In other words, focus on Jesus Christ by believing and studying the Bible. That focus will compel you to serve Him in preparation for His return.

4 Life

We serve a Trinitarian God. This means that He is three distinct persons that coexist simultaneously. God the Father, God the Son, and God the Holy Spirit are all one. God created us with three distinct parts as well. Our trichotomy consists of a body, soul, and spirit.

> ...we house four distinct conditions that influence purpose in our lives: daughter, sister, wife, and mother.

These three parts coexist simultaneously and work together. God's "home" is the church, and according to the New Testament, we are the church; therefore, His home is in us on earth. Women are the homebuilders of life. As homebuilders and temples of the Holy Spirit, we have such an opportunity to glorify the Lord as we walk in our purposes.

A woman's purpose in life is such a hot topic and is varied, yet I do believe we house four distinct conditions that influence purpose in our lives: daughter, sister, wife, and mother. As women, we glorify the Lord as we function and add value to these conditions.

Daughter

Thinking about myself as a daughter, I notice that I look just like both parents. When I am standing by my dad alone, people comment, "You look just like your dad," and when beside my mom, they say, "You and your mom look just alike." I think it is interesting that being a daughter is most evident when you resemble your parents. When a daughter is with a parent and they do not have distinct physical characteristics of that parent, it is not as obvious that the child is the biological offspring, although they very well could be. Recognizing your daughter-gene means you have also considered how you are yielded to your Creator.

Being a daughter suggests that you are a replica of someone and being led by someone. The characteristic of *daughter* signifies the sole relationship between you and the Creator. The daughter is solely responsible for pleasing the Father. Psalms 45: 10-11 states, "Hear, O daughter, consider, submit, and consent to my instruction: forget also your own people and your father's house; so will the King desire your beauty; because He is your Lord, be submissive and reverence and honor Him." In other words, this scripture says, "Girl, think, give up, and agree with the Lord's instruction. It doesn't matter where you come from. Your Father is captivated by your beauty. Honor Him by allowing your true beauty to shine because He created it." When the Lord speaks in terms of daughter, He is speaking to the replicas created as women.

Psalms 144:12 states "… That our daughters may be as pillars, sculptured in palace style." As daughters, we are graceful pillars, connected to greater strength. One definition of a *pillar* is an upright structure used for building support. One commentator suggests that daughters are godly women, wise and well-established (as a cornerstone would be fastened in a building). Daughters are united to Christ, who is the chief cornerstone. Daughters are polished with the grace of God, and they adorn the kingdom with beauty replicated from the Father.

Prayer is a daughter-like function for me. It is in these moments where I feel most like a replica of my Father. I am at a moment of zero dependence on self and 100 percent dependence on God. I meditate on His Word and pray as He leads me. This takes complete humility! Ladies, when examining your femininity, take time to think of yourself as a daughter. I know you are about to pick up three boys from school, meet your husband for dinner, and prepare for the sister-sister circle, but I encourage you to take a moment to view your life through the lens of your daughter-self. Being a daughter is a sect of womanhood that can be forgotten as life offers responsibility, but it is indeed a vital lens used to communicate to God.

Sister

Being a sister is most viewed from the perspective of our peers. To be a sister means to be a friend, a sibling, or a joint heir with someone. A sister is someone who shares the same set of parents with another or is subject to the same authority. This suggests that you are a part of a peer group in some mode. Sisterhood is a necessity for our development, as it is a more defined organization of womanhood. I do not have a biological sister, so when I think of my sisters, I think of my bridesmaids. These ladies not only agreed to be in my wedding, but they also took a vow to support my marriage. These ladies surround me and pray during milestones in my life. They grow with me and serve as some sort of accountability, walking shoulder to shoulder. How are you a sister to another? How effective are your relationships? What peer ladies do you support? Surely, Jephthah's daughter could testify about how important sisters were to her.

Judges 11:34-40 records a petite, but vital depiction, of supportive friends. Previously, Jephthah made a vow with the Lord to sacrifice a burnt offering of whatever came out of the doors of his house to meet him. He was a man of valor, and I am sure he did not expect his only child, his dancing daughter, to be that burnt offering. Indeed, she was. And as she pranced toward her father and saw him rip his clothes, she knew something was up. As a result, Jephthah's daughter (whom we will call JD) asked to go into the mountains for two months with her friends. She wanted to cry with them because she would never get married. In those times, a young lady such as JD would not have had male friends. She was an only child, and because of her final request of her father, I would assume that her friends were as close as sisters. There are many things she could have asked for, yet she desired to spend her last free days with her sisters. We are not sure what wandering or roaming looked like for JD and her friends, but it is interesting she did return to her father.

Support of a sister is geared toward goodness and accountability. Honestly, would you have encouraged JD to follow through with this seemingly unfair return? Would you have even cleared your schedule on behalf of your friend to just wander and mourn? I wonder what type of conversations the girls had on the mountain. JD may have taken this opportunity to share wisdom with her friends. Regardless, as a result, young ladies of future generations gathered yearly to commemorate her (vs. 40).

Our function as a sister is indeed the relationship that propels one to strive for better. A sister is the beautiful blade that may cut in order to purify a wound or extract an infection. That same blade can protect and destroy. To keep the blade functioning at its prime, it must be sharpened. Proverbs 27:17 says, "As iron sharpens iron, so a man sharpens the countenance of his friend." Our sister-gene is what compels us to engage in the daily tasks and processes of this life successfully. The outcome of sister or sibling relationships, whether positive or negative, will be passed along to generations. Are you active in a sisterhood legacy that represents Christ in your sphere of influence? What inheritance will you share with others?

An inheritance is not a result of what you do but more so of who you are. Because I am a child of God, through the Spirit, it is inevitable that I will have an inheritance. Humbled, Jesus called us friends (John 15:15), and His legacy resulted in eternal salvation which became our inheritance.

> Our function as a sister is indeed the relationship that propels one to strive for better.

Romans 8:17 declares that through the spirit we are "joint heirs with Christ, if indeed we suffer with Him, that we may also be glorified together." Our engagement or the lack thereof as sisters will mimic our perspective of ourselves as joint heirs with Jesus Christ. True sisters will suffer together and be honored together.

Wife

We know that to be referred to as a wife you must be joined with a man, your husband. This union is like no other and is referred to as mystical. Our wife-gene serves as a parallel of how we respond to the love of Christ. Being a wife is the only irreplaceable function for a woman. It has an appointed time for her provisions to be unveiled. This is the only function of a woman where her body is commanded to be given to another human and vice versa. Being a wife not only changes your name, but it also awakens new zones of pleasure. Sex is set aside for the wife to indulge in as recreation and procreation. *Wife* is the characteristic of a woman where her body becomes a beautiful exploration of enjoyment and pleasure. This is a safe place for our sexuality to present itself and reside. Being a wife also puts you in a different position on the battlefield. Eve was God's solution to the first issue, Adam's loneliness. Satan did not appear in the garden until the wife, Eve, existed externally. How clever is he? His goal is to distract your mission enough for you to be a counterfeit wife. I am so glad that the enemy's craftiness never trumps God's sovereignty.

> "For your Maker is your husband,
> The Lord of hosts is His name;
> And your Redeemer is the Holy One of Israel;
> He is called the God of the whole earth."

Isaiah 54:5 is one of many instances where God speaks to His people as husband. This time, Israel was forsaken as a widow and God promises to meet *her* needs as a husband would. In return, all people are viewed as wives, and this scripture reminds us that the

> Being a wife not only changes your name, but it also awakens new zones of pleasure.

Lord is the best husband we will ever have. "For I am jealous for you with godly jealousy. For I have betrothed you to one husband, that I may present you as a chaste virgin to Christ." In 1 Corinthians 11:2, Paul also uses this marital parallel between Jesus and his people to depict his duty as a friend of the Groom (aka Jesus) to establish the church. Holistically looking at humanity as a bride or wife broadens our relational perspective of the term wife. It's more than a role; it is a responsibility and opportunity to display love and reverence for the Lord.

Listening to a message I once heard Bishop T.D. Jakes suggest that a woman must be a wife prior to being pursued by her husband. When I first heard this, I was challenged, but it later birthed valuable revelation for me. Proverbs 18:22 states that, "he who finds a wife, finds a good thing and obtains favor from the Lord." This scripture gives a specific description of the type of woman he discovers and deems this a good thing. Although every wife is a woman, not every woman is seen as a wife. Proverbs 31:10 explains that finding a wife of noble character is rare and quite worthwhile.

When the Bible refers to a wife, it is referring to its original meaning of a helpmate. A wife is a helpmate who is the incomparable contributor to her husband›s comfort. She is the ultimate encourager for his journey in Christ. Likewise, a wife is a woman of purpose who can truly receive love from a man. A woman already exists as wife spiritually, and she is properly awaiting the manifestation. When a woman is aware that she is already a wife, she can prepare with purpose, instead of proposing herself to anyone. This knowledge does not restrict her singleness but allows her to fully engage in life with confidence and modesty.

Although David was anointed king early on, his role remained as shepherd for many years before he was appointed as the actual king. I believe his anointing gave him the wisdom and awareness to prepare for his new authority as he cared for the sheep. It turned his waiting into training. So, if you are single, you can rejoice in remembering that your husband is your Maker and that you are a lovely display of the Master's work. You are a wife, whether it displays itself in this lifetime or eternity. If you are married, dare to be the solution. A wife is a lady whose heart is so submitted and secure in the Lord that it is clear she is already spoken for. Watching a woman's lifestyle, there should be no question as to who her covering is and who she is intimate with.

Mother

I recently gave birth to a charismatic lady child whom we named Chloe Madison. This was an experience that words could not describe. Science has terms and structural logic to describe the birthing process, but I am convinced that it is just a miracle. Although there are books and endless resources about labor and delivery, it is still an attempt to describe God. What an honor to be selected to give birth! Think about how Christ-like giving birth can truly be. We go through about nine months of pregnancy, preparing others and ourselves for this grand arrival. People can see our transformation and truly believe. On D-Day, we endure all this pain and pressure on the behalf of someone who really has no idea, and better yet, didn't even ask for it. Now after the delivery, it's time to commission discipleship.

Jesus even uses the phrase "born again" to describe His gift of salvation. Nicodemus was a ruler of the Jews and was a bit confused about this phrase, "born again." This was probably because his only understanding of being born was being delivered by a woman, his mom. Jesus explains that this new birth is not of the flesh, but a rebirth of the Spirit "…that whosoever believes in Him should not perish but have everlasting life."

Yeshua is a Hebrew term that means "Lord of Deliverance." This name is close to the name Jesus. Jesus is our Savior, and the term savior has the same meaning as deliverer. As women, we can be deliverers like Christ through our mother-gene. We get to bring forth life! Men must partake in the creation of a child, but they cannot give birth. The mother is the giver of salvation to the world, as seen

> Do not downgrade your assignments from God because they are sources of something valuable for another.

in Mary. She gave birth to God, the Son. Mary was the human source and deliverer of salvation for the world in the flesh. That made her a mother. If you are unable to physically give birth to children, that does not deplete your instinct to mother; every woman has the ability to mother. This trait is not dependent on your physical ability but your spiritual availability and submission.

As a woman, you are equipped to deliver and to be the source that brings forth human life here on earth. You have nourishment for the survival of humans who are born and born again. Exercising your authority as a mother is, in my opinion, the most distinct. Stir up this gift inside of you. Surrender to the Lord and let Him use you. Do not downgrade your assignments from God because they are sources of something valuable for another. Mary accepted her assignment and was forever changed as she mothered the Savior of the world.

Functioning as a mother can be seen in opportunities to lead, mentor, and pastor. When searching for a career or in pursuit of perfecting a craft, a helpful tool is the assistance of a mentor or role model who is currently operating in that arena. We absorb so much from simply watching this individual. A mentor relationship, at its root, is based on a meaningful learning process. Truly relying on the Word of God in these relationships puts us in the position to supply nourishment, that which is necessary for life, health, and growth. Author Karen Ehman wrote the following:

> "I think women, especially those with children in our lives, can sometimes feel like modern-day shepherds. We certainly do our fair share of feeding, watering, prodding, protecting, nursing, encouraging and watching out for anything that might harm our lambs. At times our job is also dirty, and sometimes unpleasant, with very few 'atta girls' or social recognition. Yet it is also significant."

Just reading this statement, one can hardly imagine a world functioning without a woman as mother beyond the role of birthing. Although a mother does not always get the credit for what she does, it is undeniable that with every great circumstance, there is a mother to thank. Without nourishment, the world would only be full of potential, lacking the actual. Our role as mother, literally or spiritually, surely honors a characteristic of the Lord.

Being dressed, ready for service, and true to your womanhood will cease people's ability to categorize you. As we grow in Christ, we display the full value of our role as replicas (daughters), joint heirs (sisters), comforters (wife), and deliverers (mothers). There are *four lives* campaigning for our attention and care daily, and we must commit to their functions.

Allow me to introduce one of the many movements I promote: Dresses-4-life (D4L). What is it? Dresses-4-Life is a commitment statement or standard that says, "I am purposefully feminine." In our culture today, wearing a dress tactfully screams out "I am a lady." With this movement, I simply encourage women to wear a dress to an ordinary or routine occasion, such as to work, to class, to the grocery store, to the park, or on a road trip as a friendly reminder that being a woman is fashionable!

So, if you decide to join my Dresses-4-Life movement, you can start by agreeing to wear a dress on Wednesdays for the next month. Journal about your experiences and share it with others as you find your strength in your femininity. You can also join my social networks and share your experiences there.

In Reflection:

1. In what ways does your life reflect you are living for God? In what ways do you need to improve in being dressed and ready for "God-duty"?

2. As a daughter, how do you resemble your earthly parents? How do you resemble your heavenly Father?

3. As a sister or joint heir to the throne, how do you share in the sufferings of others and encourage them to strive for better in tough situations?

4. A wife provides comfort as a helpmate to her husband and is the ultimate encourager for his journey in Christ. If you are a wife, give some examples of how you fulfill those roles. If not yet a wife here on earth, how are you focusing your attention on God as your husband?

5. In the role of mother, whether literally or spiritually, what are your greatest challenges? What are your greatest accomplishments? What changes might you do to be more open to God's leading?

Chapter 6
Girlfriends

I love getting my hair done! It is therapy to my folli-cles. I wish insurance would qualify the hair salon as a proactive health plan. I sometimes wish it took longer to wash my hair because I could sit in that chair overnight as the stylist shampoos and massages my scalp. I never get any elaborate style. I could just leave after she conditions my hair because I feel like I've gotten my money's worth at that point. Even though I love getting my hair washed, I mostly visit a salon because it is time to get my hair trimmed. While getting the trim, I always wonder if she is cutting too much hair. I call myself trying to keep my length, but the reality is that I just get used to the split ends. I am even deceived to believe that the split ends are a vital part of me when truthfully, they are just malnourished hairs that do not pro-mote positive growth. Once the ends of your hair split, the only choice is to cut them. Split ends cannot be healed. You can only buy products to help the hair appear healthier. If the split ends re-main, over time the split will rise and damage more than the end of your hair. My split ends, which I used to value as additive length, are only fake accessories that I do not need at all.

As I was reflecting on this at the hair salon, it made me think of other things that we, as women, hold on to that only ex-ist as dead weight. This is a reason why the writer of Hebrews encourages us to "lay aside every weight and the sin that so eas-ily ensnares us." Not only does the scripture say, "get it off of you," but it also says to run with endurance. So, don't just lay stuff down, you need to move on, girl! This is even true for the perspectives we have about ourselves and others. It includes how we view other women in our lives.

Because of past hurts due to betrayal, jealousy, bullying, gossip, or abandonment to name a few, we buy into a perspective about female relationships that easily entangles us. Believing that female relationships are not vital is like keeping the split ends of your hair. Excuses are made and treatments provide temporary containment, but the split ends will continue to produce negative growth unless they are simply laid aside and cut off. Sometimes we just need a good hair trimming so our curls can bounce and play their part as we strut this runway called life.

One of the best ways to ensure your feminine health with accountability and trimmings is to surround yourself with true girlfriends! There has even been some research that suggests that having female friendships is a biological need for women. Researchers believe that women who have strong social ties to a community of women live longer than those without. *The Tending Instinct*, by Shelley E. Taylor, is a book that suggests that instead of the traditional "flight or fight" response to stress (which is mostly a male characteristic), women respond with the need to protect their children and be with friends. Dove conducted a recent study that denoted 70 percent of women felt prettier because of their female friendships.

I must say that I have the best girlfriends ever! I truly count this as a blessing. There's a saying that good friends are hard to find, and I feel like I am living in abundance. My *bestest*, Tara, is a true and rare gem. Do you remember

> One of the best ways to ensure your feminine health with accountability and trimmings is to surround yourself with true girlfriends!

that saying about the difference between good friends and true friends? It says that a good friend will be there to bail you out of jail, while a true friend would most likely be in jail with you. That is Tara Martin, literally! She was my partner in crime and now in Christ! We have so many memories and continue to make new ones.

Girlfriends

The TV show *Girlfriends* displays different women. Although it is not biblically based, it shows a key point of sisterhood: relationship. This sitcom was a comedy-drama that aired from 2000-2008. There were four main ladies who starred in this show: Joan, Toni, Mya, and Lynn, and they all had issues.

Joan and Toni met as children growing up. Joan met Lynn in college and later met Mya while working at a law firm. Joan is the source of the group as she is the central connection for everyone. Although she continually has relationship issues with men, she is constantly involved in drama, positive or negative, with her girlfriends.

Toni is outspoken and self-centered. Deep down, she is ashamed of who she truly is and what she truly desires. She equates money to success and worth and is motivated by her ego.

Mya is the sassy assistant to Joan and later housewife and author. She was first despised by Toni, who considered her friendship as lower class. Mya is from a different socioeconomic background than the group; her speech, comments, and characterization portray her as being from the "hood."

Lynn is depicted as the most sexually adventurous of the bunch and is driven by her free-spirited personality. She has a fear of commitment but has a niche for learning as she obtained five graduate degrees.

We can look at the character flaws in each woman or view the unit of sisterhood as fulfillment! Each lady has a vital strength for the other, and this is discovered as they grow more intimately as sisters. The show displays, in its own way of course, *how* much we truly need each other. If a female lacks a sisterhood, she may fill that void with something contrary to her purpose.

A community of women is a sisterhood and is a great visual of our purpose. Ecclesiastes 4:9 puts it simply in saying that two are better that one. Engaging in female relationships can be most edifying. Not only are you around individuals who share your anatomy,

If you are ever searching for your purpose, start by admitting that you are female.

but also your purpose. I believe that everyone has a specific (as well as a generic) purpose and calling on their lives. If you are ever searching for your purpose, start by admitting that you are female. That very revelation will point you down the right avenue to the desired you. God created us in His image, some male and female, and meditating on this truth does not limit you. It will free you to be you, an instrument of God.

Sister Circle

When I mention sisterhood, I am not only talking about friendships with the women you know. I am referring to any woman. It's easy to care for the women you know, but what about the women you've never met? How are you able to call her sister?

Ephesians 4 says we are many members and one body. That means that as a body of Christ, we are connected by Christ. We have been reconciled to our Father. There are at least six dynamic women mentioned in Exodus 1 and 2 who all supported each other simply by being uniquely themselves. They give us great insight into a sisterhood that occurs between a group of what seems like unrelated women.

The children of Israel were living in the will of the Lord, being fruitful and increasing abundantly. Due to their prosperity, the King of Egypt made the Israelites slaves and put them to work to build his kingdom. The officials saw that the harsher they treated the people, the more they grew and multiplied. The king even spoke to the Hebrew midwives, specifically Shiphrah and Puah, and requested that if a male child was born, he should be killed. These were some rough solutions due to a simple fear.

As a result of Shiphrah and Puah's fear of God, they refused to do as the king commanded. These two women, although they were not giving birth at the time, certainly were making a pro-life stance in their actions, and God was pleased. The Lord blessed them with families of their own. This reminds me of the three Hebrew boys in Daniel 3 who refused to bow to the commands of King Nebuchadnezzar. They put their lives in danger for their faith, and their faith is what saved them.

Because of two brave midwives walking in their purpose, the people multiplied and grew in great numbers. Simply living a life of integrity and purpose will set you up to contribute to sisterhood in ways you may never see. Your decisions and reactions to situations will plant seeds of sisterhood for generations to come. Due to the midwives' actions, Pharaoh made his sneaky objective public.

Exodus 2 continues with this sisterhood story by introducing Moses' family. His mom hid him and then placed him along the bank of the Nile in an effort to save his life. His sister continued to watch him and approached the scene when needed. Moses' mother reminds me of how Abraham took Isaac to the mountain to sacrifice him. To the natural eye, what he was doing could seem ludicrous, but due to his faith, God provided a ram in the bush. I wonder what Moses' mother was thinking that compelled her to abandon her son. The scripture says that when she saw he was a fine child, she hid him for three months before releasing him. Her actions not only saved her son but also blessed another woman. Pharaoh's own daughter was moved with compassion and gathered Moses from the bank.

Sometimes it is the radical faith we operate in that contributes to developing sisterhood. Sometimes the ladies who you are jealous of, the ladies who get on your nerves, or the ladies you perceive as your enemies will be your greatest allies.

Pharaoh's daughter went against the grain in many ways. She decided to become a single mother. The text did not say she was married, so I would guess having a child at her age could cause issues when a man wanted to pursue her. She could have thought about that fact or the fact that this child was of another race. She was Egyptian, and the child was Hebrew, just like the people who were slaves to her family. Pharaoh's daughter just followed her compassion despite the potential stumbling blocks. Although I am sure her goal was not sisterhood, it turned out to be a beautiful connection.

> Sometimes it is the radical faith we operate in that contributes to developing sisterhood.

In Pharaoh's daughter's attempt to properly care for this child, she did not reject help. Sometimes we unveil true sisterhood by not only reaching out to help others but by allowing our sister to celebrate and rejoice with us. Instead of being stubborn and prideful, she allowed another to aid her in rescuing this baby. Miriam, Moses' sister, kept watch of her brother and was able to reconnect her family as her mom was now able to nurse and bond with her son. Have you ever gotten paid to do what you would do for free? That's how Moses' mom had to feel. Sisterhood is not always about what you have the choice to do. Sometimes it's about declaring that you have no other choice but to live in purpose with integrity, exercise radical faith, and seek help from others.

Being an instrument of God produces a lasting impression. Each instrument is unique, and there are different sections or categories according to the material it is made of. In high school and college, I played the clarinet, which is considered a woodwind instrument because of the way the sound is produced. Single reed instruments such as clarinets and saxophones produce sound by putting air through a mouthpiece. This causes a reed to vibrate and make sound. A brass instrument, on the other hand, produces sound through lip vibrations. As women of diverse gifting and passions, we are all called to operate in one orchestra conducted by the Lord. To me, this is sisterhood at its best. As we walk in obedience to God, the sounds we produce will not only be for solo significance, but it will blend in harmony with other sisters in Christ.

Now the question is, "Do we create girlfriends or are they just solely organic?" I believe friendships happen naturally, and the only way we obtain these relationships is by agreeing that they are of value. Decide today to value your female relationships. Be of value to your girlfriends, knowing that these relationships are imperative for your development. If you are saying, "I don't have good relationships with other women," I would challenge you to examine yourself and find the core belief that is fostering this thought. I have a friend who simply prayed for female relationships, and God granted her the request in ways she could not imagine. Prayer is as organic as it gets.

In Reflection:

1. Consider your circle of friends and the women in your life. Do you have women you can count on no matter what? If so, what do you appreciate most about them and the relationships? If not, what steps do you need to begin taking so you can develop close friendships?

2. What female attributes in other women do you admire most and why? What female attributes do you have that might benefit your sisterhood? For example, are you an encourager or do you have the gift of hospitality?

3. Reflect on a time when you witnessed women in the body of Christ working together to honor God. What about their unique gifts and personalities all coming together made it so beautiful?

4. Have you been witness to a time when women didn't work together to honor God? If so, how did that work out and what might have been done differently?

5. Female friendships are great ways to have accountability, spiritual counsel, and support. What are some other ways you see that female friends would be an asset? Think about which ones are most important to you and how you've been blessed by friends. Pray and thank God for these relationships and ask how you may contribute toward making them even stronger.

Chapter 7

Busy Resting

Busy Times

She got on my nerves! She took control of my life, rushed me, and was just plain rude. I could not understand why she was so nasty to me. I tried to be friendly, but it just would not work out. Although *time* is not a human, these thoughts express how I would feel about "her" if she were. I am pretty sure I could not be friends with time as a human. Can you tell that *time* is my growing pain?

Growing up, the actual, correct time was never displayed in my home. Every clock in the house said something different. In the living room, there was a clock mounted on the wall above the door frame headed toward the kitchen, and it read 12:20 p.m., while the digital clock on the coffee table displayed 12:07 p.m. If you were standing in the living room, looking at the round black wall clock, the kitchen clock was in your forward vision tick-tocking at 12:15 p.m. Let's not forget the digital clock built into the stove, with its bold, red numbers screaming **11:59 a.m.** Although I felt deceived, it was my mother›s method for keeping everyone on time. Contradiction was at its greatest. My room was my only sense of true time. Only in my room was where the truth of the time dwelled. To this very day, I cannot stand when any clock is set five minutes fast. I should send around a petition about this. Why do we do such things? Why is deception so productive?

In 2010, I could not stand the phrase "If I had time …" It was sickening to me because it frequently erupted in my vocabulary. I kept having to use the phrase, "I don't have time" until finally I believed it. I found myself living by time, which to me is different from having an agenda. An agenda is simply a to-do list in some type of order. I often found myself consumed by the amount of time I had to carry out a plan rather than the plan itself. If you know me. you know I LOVE to be on time (even though it's not always the norm for my life). I get a rush when it comes to planning and I have to force myself not to purchase a new calendar when I am only in the middle of the year. I'm sure you're familiar with the saying your gift can be your curse.

God had to really remind me that He's sovereign. Time is His. It was that moment that I relaxed. I relinquished control and looked around at the sovereignty of the Lord. I remember asking God for peace about the time, and it was as if I spent five hours seeking Him, but only thirty minutes on the clock had passed. I was amazed and began my campaign. Any time I felt overwhelmed, I quoted my slogan, "God is sovereign, God controls the time." Girl, you would not believe how helpful that was and continues to be! I truly believe that the tongue has the power of life and death. I also believe that when we speak, both happen—life and death. It is just our focus that drives our emotional reaction to that truth.

> Practically, a great way to manage what you do with the time is to develop SMART Goals.

My campaign, "God is sovereign, God controls the time," breathes life to my peace of mind and death to bad stress. The literal term "time management" is a myth. This is a sobering thought for me. I admire order and am quite organized, but no matter how organized I am, the twenty-four-hour day stays consistent. I cannot change the time; I can just manage what *I* do with the time.

Practically, a great way to manage what you do with the time is to develop SMART Goals. A goal is your target objective or result. I believe that setting goals that are **SMART**: Specific, **M**easurable, **A**ttainable, **R**elevant, and **T**ime-bound can put you in a position to discern what God is doing in your life. Ask the Lord, "What time is it in my life?" In other words, assess your personal season and manage it accordingly. Do not be deceived by jealousy, judgments, and false images. Find your quiet place, where truth dwells, and allow God to reveal *your* time.

Busy At Home

Destiny was the name of a woman's group which I led within DURAG Ministries, that catered to the ladies from ages twenty-two to thirty. In 2009, the theme for Destiny was "Busy at Home." This was the first year we started destiny dinners with the purpose of exposing our ladies to other godly women in the community. We met once a month at the home of an older woman. These women were happy to host us as they provided biblical wisdom to our table topics and fed us physical and spiritual food. What they may not have realized is that what ministered to us the most was being in their homes. Because we were a group of young, unmarried women living in new apartments with friends, just being in a loving, mature home was edifying. The home is a place where memories are created and where theories take root.

Titus 2:4-5 says that when the older women train the younger women to be busy at home (along with other things), the Word of God will not be blasphemed. That is huge! To blaspheme means to speak evil of, or irreverently of God's name. It is so easy to get into the habit of saying "Oh my God" when something surprising happens, with zero true reverence to God.

Collin Smith wrote an insightful book about the Ten Commandments called *The 10 Greatest Struggles of Your Life*, and he suggested that our greatest calling as a body of believers is to honor the Lord's name through our actions, as well as our talk. Blasphemy is the opposite of that. Blasphemy also happens when claims are made, such as, "The Lord led me to ..." and He did not. When these claims occur, sadly, you are attempting to steal God's glory and His honor. When wise women mentor younger women, teaching them to be busy at home, they are developing a community of young women who honor the name of Christ. Ultimately, older women are charged to be taught and then teach sound doctrine to younger women, with emphasis on loving their husbands and children, being self-controlled and pure, being busy at home, being kind, and submitting to their husbands.

Being busy at home is not only about cleaning, cooking, and moving around the house. It is about the heart. You know the saying, "home is where the heart is." The home is such a practical place to minister God's love. Think about your home growing up. What type of memories resided in your home? What emotions were stirred when you reflect on your home? Did you ever have a place you would sincerely call home? Think about the influence that home or lack of a home had on your development.

I have many memories when I think of home, good and bad. Some memories I want to travel with me as traditions, while other memories cause me to pray against generational curses. The home is a vital place, and we can have a sphere of influence right where we are. If you are thinking, *When I get married, I will begin to be busy at home,* I want you to consider it now. Take some time to clean your house, apartment, dorm, or room. While you are cleaning or organizing, ask the Lord to do the same in your heart. Ask Him to cleanse, purge, and create order within you and write about the experience.

Have you allowed unwelcomed strangers (impure thoughts, doubts, and fears) into your home? Be reminded that you are the manager of this house, and you have the authority! God gave you the keys a long time ago, so use them to lock and unlock doors in order to honor the name of the Lord.

The Shunammite woman found in 2 Kings 4:8-37 knew all about being busy at home. She had a great gift of hospitality and was a notable wife. Providing food and shelter were key components of her gifting. She was not just doing what people call "woman's work"; this was her ministry. She could not help but to create the space for the presence of God to dwell. As a result of her service, she was blessed with a child. With this blessing, her faith was indeed tested.

Have you ever wanted something so bad that you were afraid to ask for it? You could hardly pray about it because your thoughts kept getting sidetracked to the future view of you with it. It takes over your everyday living and molds your perspective on life. When someone asks what you want, you do not even utter it because everyone has counted you out. The scripture did not say that the Shunammite woman wanted a child this badly, but I could just imagine how badly this barren woman wanted a child to carry her legacy. In fact, when Elisha told her that she would embrace a son the next year, she could not even believe it. But it was true, and she conceived.

Be busy at home by creating the space in your heart for God to dwell. When this happens, you have to be ready to receive blessings and reject fear. Creating the space should occur with high expectations for situations to be powerful and living!

Although the Shunammite woman created the space as a duty to the Lord, she had to use the space for her son to be healed. Her son died in her lap. When this happened, she placed him in the room she created and went to find the prophet to heal him. She demonstrated her faith when she returned to that space with her dilemma, instead of burying it.

Being busy at home is a matter of creating the space for the presence of God to rule in your home and heart. In that space, you will be blessed, and your faith will be tested, but hold fast to the faith. Allow that space/moment/thought to be the pasture that the Lord leads you to for rest as David explained in Psalm 23.

Finally, be busy at home through prayer. Rahab was busy at home when she decided to assist the spies and believe in the one true God (Joshua 2). As a result of Jael being busy at home, she put a peg through the head of the leader of the army (Judges 4). Hannah was busy at home with her husband conceiving the son she prayed for who grew to be a great judge, prophet, and priest (Samuel 1). Because you value and understand the charge to be busy at home, you, too, have a winning story to complete.

When you are making decisions, I would encourage you to always think about your home first. Start at your core and foundation. Always ask yourself two questions: "What would Jesus do?" and "How would He encourage a woman to do it?"

Beauty Rest

As I stated previously, as a child and even now I had an enchanted imagination. I remember telling people my father was a doctor. Again, this is still in debate depending on your definition of *doctor*, but surely he was and is not a medical doctor. It made so much sense to me though. Because my mother worked night shifts, my dad had to be the medical expert. I remember being sick in my bed, and my dad would say, "Doctor Dad is on his way." He would make me eat chicken noodle soup and drink lots of juice. I always had to stay under the blankets and "sweat it out," and if I was not feeling better soon afterward, he would put his magical hand on my forehead and say, "Heal her, Lord." That was the best part. I would laugh and repeat, "Heal me, Lord," and sure enough, I would feel better and fall sound asleep in my father's arms. Although this was his way of making fun of the situation, it stuck with me. Having childlike faith is a cherished characteristic that Jesus adores. It's the kind of faith that lives on every word of the Father. This faith allows for the most beautiful rest.

In Luke 10:42, Luke records the popular story about Martha and Mary where Jesus made the famous statement (famous for my life) "But one thing is needed ..." This statement has troubled me and taught me the most about myself at the same time. I am learning from Mary these days because I think I may have mastered Martha in past seasons of my life. Martha was the sister who had things under control. She welcomed Jesus into her home, yet Jesus said that Mary "has chosen that good part," so I figure she had some insight that Martha lacked. Mary seemed to be a receiver, and Martha was a giver. Both are vital characteristics, but why would Jesus say that Mary chose the good part?

In order to receive the best beauty rest, one must recognize the good part, which is the presence of God. Jesus is where we find rest. Exodus 20:8 says "Remember the Sabbath and keep it holy." This is one of the most neglected and overlooked Commandments. Many times, it just seems completely irrelevant to our relationship with Christ. Recognizing or honoring the Sabbath is vital because it brings a balance of worship and stewardship. It helps us remember that Jesus does the work, not us. Jesus empowers us to act on His behalf through the Holy Spirit, but if we neglect His presence, we will lack the confidence of the inner workings of Christ in our lives. Not honoring the Sabbath is ultimately disobeying one of the Commandments. It seems that Mary in Luke 10:42 has chosen to keep the Commandment of remembering the Sabbath by choosing the good part.

> Having childlike faith is a cherished characteristic that Jesus adores.

Jesus tells us in Matthew 11:28, "Come to Me, all you who labor and are heavy laden, and I will give you rest." This is not just doing things for the sake of Christ, rather, it is being in the presence of Christ. What Martha was doing was not wrong until it became a distraction from what was currently needed. At this point what was a distraction became a burden, and Martha asked for the wrong thing. "Lord, do You not care that my sister has left me to serve alone? Therefore tell her to help me." Jesus responds, "Martha, Martha, you are worried and troubled about many things. But one thing is needed, and Mary has chosen that good part, which will not be taken away from her" (Luke 10:40-42). The scripture did not state that Mary did not help at all; it just says that Mary came to Jesus, as Matthew 11:28 encourages us to.

Heavy laden or burdened people are those who are worried and distracted by life's to-do list. The worry and distractions keep us from choosing the good part. Ladies, if you are living without peace of mind and constantly under stress, my question to you is, "Are you choosing the beauty of rest that comes from Christ?" I know things get tough, and it seems like there is never enough time to get everything done, and what seems right becomes a distraction or a burden that causes us to miss the opportunities to sit at the feet of Christ. It is important that we all recognize we still need our beauty rest.

When you have taken this invitation for Jesus" yoke, you ultimately signed up for Christ to supply your beauty rest that you might be busy resting. This type of rest is incomparable, and others will notice. They will look at your life and wonder how you do it all. How do you balance an active life and look so lovely doing it? As they see what would seem to be low moments in your life, they will not be able to disregard the true light that continues to shine, pointing to Christ. You just have to let them know that you have chosen the good part—beauty rest.

Being About My Father's Business

In this last section, I would like to close on a personal note. I have found that busy resting is best captured when we are about our Father's business. As a child in first grade, I remember having my first job. Yes, I was working at an early age. I worked after school. My dad would pick me up every day in his gray automatic Isuzu (i-zoozoo, as I called it). I would run to him with excitement because I knew my real life was about to begin. I was that kid who had it all figured out. I *knew* my parents only had me in school because it was the law.

My real life began when I climbed in that truck. Our first stop was at Burger King where I had to get my darling Whopper Jr. with cheese. We, my dad and I, believed I worked better on a full stomach. (Now that my husband and I no longer eat meat, my dad often reminds me that I used to love cheeseburgers.) We'd leave the drive-thru and we'd be off! At the time, my dad worked for some delivery company. I mean, *we* worked, and we had to go get packages and deliver them to companies. This was my first job. I was a delivery girl! I never questioned why I worked with my father or even if it was supposed to be happening. I never once questioned my ability or qualification for this position. I never asked about my mother, grandma, or my brother during this time. All that really mattered was that I was with my father—nothing else—just being about my father's business.

Once we finished eating, I proceeded to tell my dad every detail about my school day. I had nothing to hide, and he wanted all the details. He would listen and respond to everything. Sometimes, I would even say, "Hey Dad, how was your day?" and ask him, "What is our plan for today?" At times, he would look at me and laugh, *as if I was not the one responsible for completing the work or something.* He would eventually let me know where we were going to deliver the next package. I never really had a clue what he was talking about, because most of the time, I had never been there; but it didn't matter really because I trusted him. All my security was in the fact that I was with my dad. I would always reply, "OK, Pop, let's hit it." That simply meant that I was ready to continue with my father's business.

As we traveled, I knew I was working hard when my dad let me work the stick shift. I would sit tall in the passenger seat and shift the gear stick. This was the most important task in my line of work because my daddy needed me to pay close attention to the sound so I would know when to go to the next gear. I had to watch the road as well to be prepared to slow to a stop and put the gear in neutral or park. I remember asking my dad, "What if I mess up?" He laughed again. I didn't think that was funny at all because my job was significant. My dad would simply say "Bae, as long as you are with me, you can't mess up." I had no question about that and kept doing my job while chatting with my father.

When we walked into the companies, my job was now to remain quiet because my father was going to do all the talking. Even as a first grader, I knew it was unprofessional to speak unless spoken to or given permission by my father. The times I did make suggestions was when the orange soda I drank with my Whopper Jr. started taking over my six-year-old bladder. Because I was on the job, I only told my dad that I had to use the bathroom when we were back in the truck and on the road again. I didn't want to practice bad business, but for some reason, we would always have to loop back and use their restroom anyway. Finally, one day my father told me, "Bae, when you need to use the restroom, just ask me right away." After that work assessment, I had a better under-standing of the terms of my job. Although he told me to speak up, my father started asking me if I had to use the restroom before I could even say anything, and he always knew when I had to go! We were such a good team, my father and me. I was glad my dad was able to help me work.

Reflecting on this childhood experience, the Heaven-ly Father taught me some valuable lessons through my dad. He taught me to always be about the Father's business. Being about His business, I know He will lead and comfort me. Developing an intimate relationship with Him is vital. My Father will always provide and never let the job fail, as He corrects and encourages me along the journey. Although my part was important, He is in control.

He taught me to never forsake on-the-job training and make my request of Him, full of faith, when in need. Most of all, the Lord taught me that all things work out for the good "for those who love God and are called according to His purpose" (Romans 8:28). I encourage you to reflect on these lessons and rejoice in your paradigm shifts as you are being about your Father's busi-ness, ultimately being busy resting.

In Reflection::

1. Do you find yourself feeling controlled by time or do you feel you have some control over it?

2. What are some practical steps you can take to have more control over your time?

3. Making room for God in your home plays a key role in striking balance. Do you consistently make room for God in your home life and heart? What are some ways you can open up more room for God?

4. Reflect on all your priorities. Are you going about your Father's business or do adjustments need to be made? What are they?

5. In today's culture, finding time to rest in God's love and focus on Him seems to be a challenge. What are some things you can do to rest more in God's love? How do you think it will impact your life?

Chapter 8
Healthy Bodies, Healthy Babies

"May God Himself, the God of peace, sanctify you through and through. May your whole spirit, soul and body be kept blameless at the coming of our Lord Jesus Christ. The one who called you is faithful and he will do it."
1 Thessalonians 5:23-24 (NIV)

*H*ealthy bodies, healthy babies is the phrase I kept repeating aloud when working out with the insane Shaun T. (in my living room with the DVD of course). The workout is a beast, so I had to motivate myself. Becca joined me and signed up for the healthy bodies, healthy babies' movement, and together we would scream this phrase to get though those concluding globe jumps. Although this saying was fun and physically true, I believe it reigns on all health levels. When you take the time to exercise your mind, you will tone and define an important muscle, the brain. That's why it was so helpful to say the motivational phrase aloud! Again, if you are not careful, you will be in the midst of a workout/in the midst of life and say out of your mouth, "This is too hard, I will not be able to finish." The moment you do that is the moment you start modifying the exercise. Compromise in your life becomes more appealing. Life can be like a workout. The positive results of your grind will far exceed your current discomfort.

As He Increased, I Decreased

So, weight seems to be a touchy subject. For me, weight was who I was. I've always been a larger lady, never small in frame. It's so crazy that I have such a visible stature, yet I am such a behind-the-scenes person at heart. I think God is just a comedian. Growing up I was always the tallest; large and in charge! I believe I've been the same height since 8th grade (5'8 ½"), and I have worn the same shoe size (10 ½ or 11) since then as well. I've always been a plus-size model. Coming to college, most people throw around the phrase "gaining the freshman fifteen." Well, I do not know if it was the fact that JMU is in the mountains or not, but I lost ten pounds my freshman year. It was amazing. I have to say that I felt really good about myself. The coolest part was that the weight loss wasn't intentional. I started working out at UREC because I had to for class credit. When I went to D-hall, I ate salads and fruit because it was an option, and I actually enjoy healthy food.

The coolest thing for me was to realize that my walk with Christ mirrored my walk with my physical health. It was the same. During my freshman year, I started attending a Bible study because I thought it was the right thing to do. I grew up going to church, but I would say I was a cultural Christian. I had the information and the mother who yelled, "Get up Cherelle, you gonna be late for church," although it was 9:30 a.m. and church was a total of five minutes away on a slow day and started at 11 a.m. But I cannot say that I truly pursued a relationship with Christ. It's like living in the house with your family, but not really knowing your heritage or who you truly come from. My college experience was my activation experience with the Lord. I am such a fan of college ministries! Anyway, I was going to Bible study, and I started to hunger and thirst for righteousness, by accident. I read my Bible and *enjoyed* learning.

My sophomore year is when my spiritual growth was expedited while my weight declined. I would go to the track at Memorial Hall (before the baseball field was there) and run while listening to some great empowering Christian music. I remember specifically listening to "Yes" by Shekinah Glory while running. At the end of that song, I realized I ran double of what I wanted with water streaming down my face. I would like to think it was sweat, but yes, it was tears. It was then that I realized I had an encounter with God during my workout! That was and is so powerful for my life. To this day, I dedicate my workouts to the Lord. I feel so refreshed after a nice run; I get much-needed meditation and prayer time during them. I know if it's been a while between workouts, I need to check my prayer life. I've recently learned that when I only snack on the Word of God, I overeat in the natural, so I had to challenge myself to *feast* on His Word.

I do not tell this story to boast on my weight loss but rather to boast on the goodness of Christ. He is a supernatural God, but He does communicate in natural ways. He relates to us. I wonder what was Jesus" workout plan? What if He did pushups when He was praying in the garden? I mean, it says He was bleeding. What if Jesus was using a tree to do pull-ups right before the transfiguration? Ha! And what about when He washed the disciples' feet? He may have been doing crunches on the floor when He gave Himself the revelation. We know He didn't do water aerobics, but He did walk on water, so I am assuming his calf muscles were ripped (like my husband's). Ask the Lord to help you work out your life in the way He designed you to. What is your workout plan? Good health is employing a balance between the physical, mental, and spiritual being of yourself.

> When we speak things, our brain makes copies and files those words.

Healthy Speaking

"You are what you eat." Remember that saying? Well, I believe that to be true, three-fold: spiritually, physically, and mentally. What you believe is who you can become. If you truly believe that you are unattractive, unfortunately, you will create that truth for yourself. Negative self-talk is not a healthy snack. Proverbs 18:21 states, "Death and life are in the power of the tongue, and those who love it will eat its fruit." The ability to speak with power is a direct characteristic of our Creator. Whether you know it or not, your words and thoughts have creative power. Your brain certainly agrees with this, and so should your heart. When we speak things, our brain makes copies and files those words.

Has your mood or a perceived circumstance ever inspired you to prepare for your day by saying, "This is not going to be a good day"? The moment you spoke that, you made a declaration to yourself. Your brain starts working by making copies or memories. Some things honestly seem horrible, but that does not change your ability to speak life in those situations. Genesis 1:2 states that the earth was "void," but God took that as an opportunity to speak life, literally. A healthy snack would be allowing God to tame your tongue. James 3:2 (NIV) says that "Anyone who is never at fault in what they say is perfect, able to keep his whole body in check." In other words, what you say will affect the entire body. Matthew 12:35 states that "The good man brings good things out of the good stored up in him, and the evil man brings evil things out of the evils stored in him." Speak what is true. Give attention to the good things in you and allow your brain to make carbon copies.

Healthy Thoughts

"For as he thinks in his heart, so is he..."
Proverbs 23:7

Thinking is a vital part of our being. According to science, the ability to think and make complex decisions is what separates us from animals. This is not wrong, but it is not completely true. What also separates us is the fact that we were created in the image of God and serve as His glory on earth. If your thoughts are opposite to this truth, they can very well be toxic. A *toxin* is a poisonous substance produced in living cells that cause disease. There are many methods of getting rid of toxins in your body; basically, you must avoid chemicals that cause harm, prepare your body to work properly as designed, and release stored toxins. I would propose the same method for removing toxic thoughts. Toxic thoughts are thoughts that cause disease. It may not occur immediately, but all thoughts conflicting with the will of God are poisonous. Because of Christ, we to have access to a cognitive detox.

To think in your heart simply means to truly believe. We can be exposed to information and truth, but that does not always turn into a belief in our hearts. It is toxic to read the truth—the

79

Word of God—but believe the opposite. To combat this toxin, we must meditate on God's Word and absorb it often. This spiritual discipline—meditation—can become the antivirus protection plan for your heart. Daniel gives a great example of someone thinking in his heart. Daniel 1:8 states, "but Daniel purposed in his heart that he would not defile himself ..." If you read the rest of chapter one, you will find that Daniel and his friends proceeded with a dietary discipline, and as a result, God gave them knowledge, wisdom, and skills.

Before Daniel made a plan, he purposed in his heart. In other words, he believed it inwardly, and it became so. Have you ever tried to change a habit or aspect of your life by planning first? Don't get me wrong, planning is vital to success, but it proves more effective when you first make a determination in your heart.

Healthy Eating

Do you ever wonder why the first sin was manifested through eating? Food and the woman ... the fall of Man is all attributed to a piece of fruit! That's a lot of power, right? Of course, we know that it was much more than just eating that exposed Adam and Eve. They were influenced to have alternative desires and disobeyed God. We can glean interesting cooking lessons from Eve. One is that *consuming* what is forbidden can bring sin into our worlds. I am not making a doctrinal debate here; I am simply encouraging you to watch what you eat.

Try not to over or undereat. I know it sounds simple, but I believe that the practical disciplines can render the most spiritual impacts. If you know that second bowl of banana pudding (I love it) is not necessary because you are already full and leaning over, then command yourself to stop and remove yourself from what is now temptation. Banana pudding is a blessing to me, but when it is out of place, it can be the very temptation that leads me to sin through disobedience.

Refuse to overeat on TV shows that will cause you to gossip, envy, or slander someone. Romans 1:29-30 refers to these things as wickedness, and 2 Timothy 2:19 reminds us to turn away from wickedness. Be careful; do not eat wickedness. If something is wicked, it is evil or morally bad in principle. I do not believe that the actual fruit that Adam and Eve ate was "bad for you," it was more so that they were not supposed to eat it. Purchasing that extra dress may not be bad for you, but if it is contrary to your shopping discipline, and conviction is reaching out to you, it is now an act of wickedness. The good news is that self-control is a part of the fruit of the spirit. This is the type of fruit our first couple should have eaten. Pray about and celebrate your three-fold eating (mind, body, and spirit) habits and watch the Holy Spirit operate in you.

The great commission says to make disciples of all the nations. Whether you desire to birth children physically or spiritually, your health can determine the platform of their walk. Living a healthy lifestyle is not just about how you look, although that is a factor. It is also about how you affect a community of people. Your overall health will communicate loud and clear. Allow your IronDress to sharpen that of another's. Allow your sisters to hold you accountable to healthy eating as you do the same for them. Today, decide to use your tongue as an instrument for life. Celebrate your health as you decide today to let the Lord lead you in this area of your life.

3 John 1:2 says,
"Beloved, I pray that you may prosper in all things and be in health, just as your soul prospers."

In Reflection:

1. Take time to consider your current situation and lifestyle. Identify healthy behaviors and not-so-healthy ones. What steps can you take to continue fostering the healthy behaviors and to stop doing the unhealthy ones?

2. Think of the most prominent thoughts you've had the past few hours. Were they primarily positive or negative? What does the Bible say you should think about? (I encourage you to delve into scripture for this one.)

3. How might healthy thoughts and actions impact your walk with God? What about unhealthy thoughts and actions?

4. Healthy eating provides fuel for your body to operate at an optimal level so you can honor God. How are your current eating habits contributing to honoring God? What are some ways you might improve?

5. Healthy activities stimulate your body and help maintain healthy muscles and organs, both physically and spiritually. How are your current activities contributing to a healthy body, spirit, and mind? What are some things you might want to do differently?

Chapter 9
A Single Gift

remember reading a book by Emily Ryan while in college titled, *Who has Your Heart?* This book challenged me to my core. I had to ask myself, *Cherelle, if God told you that you would never marry, would your relationship with Him be different?* At that point, I whispered *Yes* in response. But from that moment on, I made a promise with myself that I would no longer keep my gift dormant.

I responded to Christ again. In His pursuit, He not only asked me for my mind, but also for my heart, and I surrendered it daily. I titled my devotional time "Dates" and even nicknamed the Lord *Boolove*. Don't laugh at me, but I was and am wholeheartedly in a relationship with Christ. God will romance you if you let Him. His peace that surpasses understanding is a phenomenal truth and my favorite location to retreat.

Yes, we are gifts to earth from God, and I dare you to celebrate it. It's funny, I have not come across many positive greeting or special occasion cards for single ladies. Recently, I've heard that Valentine's Day has been deemed "single awareness day," and that does not sound celebratory at all. I saw an encouraging quote on Facebook that stated something to the effect of "I am not single, I am chosen." I kind of like that concept, but the truth is that you are single and chosen. Beyoncé started a new movement for this generation when she came out with her hit "Single Ladies." Although it is not a whole view of our single gift, it gives a perspective of celebrating independence and not settling.

Being successfully single is a valued feature. For some reason, to be defined as single has summed itself up to mean "I am waiting for my man." Although that may be true, it is so much more! Paul equally refers to marital and non-marital life as a gift. In 1 Corinthians 7: 7 it states, "But each one has his own gift from God, one in this manner and another in that." When Paul refers to "gift from God," it is referring to a spiritual gift like those mentioned in 1 Corinthians 12.

Considering that Paul had a Jewish background which regarded marriage as a duty, it would be contrary to his culture to regard singleness as a gift. This furthermore suggests the divine inspiration of his letters. For a woman to unveil her true identity in Christ, she must at some point celebrate her single self, regardless of her relationship status. If you are married and never had the true opportunity to establish yourself as a single gift, I believe you have to embrace that aspect at some point. This may be cause for multitasking, but it is vital to reflect on.

One of my best girlfriends, Chaka Burnett, was a great model of a lady living within her single gift. She was truly an independent woman, allowing the world to become her playground and mission field. This was only possible because of her full dependence on Jesus Christ. Chaka, previously known as Chaka Gray, is now married to her next gift and still living on purpose. In writing this section, I asked Chaka a few questions about how she kept her single gift alive and unhampered:

Chaka, you were married at the age of thirty. How did you view your single gift in that time before marriage?

"I was blessed to have people, especially women of God, in my life who often reminded me of the scripture in 1 Peter 2:9 that speaks to the fact that I was chosen, that I was royalty, the daughter of a King, and that I could stand and proclaim God's praises in the world. Their constant teachings about how God viewed me and what He thought about me gave me the courage and the confidence to go through life expecting great things. It has shaped me into the woman I am today, and those teachings will continue to shape me into exactly what God wants me to be ... the best!"

"Becoming who God intended for you to be has a lot to do with discovery, both in who you are as His daughter and who He has created you to be for the purpose of assisting others. The encouragement and wisdom of the women I was blessed to encounter throughout my life, as well as a developing relationship with God, helped me to set values and goals for my life that enabled me to live life with no regrets. Some of these lessons came from the wisdom of women who emulated what I was striving for, while others came from the tears of women who had the misfortune of learning life's lessons the hard way. All in all, their willingness to allow God to use them to help me is what I offer to you now, and hope that you will come to understand the unique situation that God put you in when He created you unapologetically female."

What jewel would you unveil to women who are striving to live out loud in their single gift?

"Girlfriend, you have power! Not just the kind of power that allows you to become famous or head of a corporation, but intimate power—the power of your femininity. Women are soft, round, and lovely. You are a unique blend of mystery, creativity, grace, and allure. You were created purposefully by design and different from a man. These are the traits that make you so appealing to a man. But your attraction is not merely your physical beauty, but it also consists of who you are spiritually. And spiritual beauty takes time to develop."

Why is celebrating singleness so important?

"Your singleness serves as the perfect caveat for this maturity to take place. It was during my singleness that I began a meaningful journey of encountering God. I decided to embrace singleness as a gift—an opportunity for exploration and personal growth. I traveled, developed relationships with friends, and engaged in many different aspects of ministry. And when I needed to steal away and spend time alone with God in prayer, reading my Word, or worship, I could do so at my leisure; and I didn't have to worry about anyone else."

"The apostle Paul tells us in 1 Corinthians 7:32-33 that unmarried individuals are concerned with pleasing God, while the married individual has to be concerned with pleasing God and a spouse. Singleness gives us the freedom to serve God without the constraints of having to divide our time, focus, and energy with a spouse. Your primary focus can be on pleasing God without worrying about neglecting your duties as a wife. It also provides ample time to learn about who you are and the things you enjoy. God can use you freely in this state because it is during this time that your heart and desire depend most on Him. As you spend time with Him exclusively and begin to allow Him to fill the void in your life, He will reveal Himself to you intimately and teach you how to be the beautiful and unique woman He created you to be."

"There are gifts and treasures and untold beauty within you, but these treasures are meant to be shared only with the one God has intended for you—the one you will marry. Song of Solomon 4:12 (NLT) says this about your precious gifts: "You are like a private garden, my treasure, my bride! You are a spring that no one else can drink from, a fountain of my own." The world will see no value in your garden if you swing the gates open carelessly."

"But rest assured, if you are a woman who has already opened her gates before, you, too, can have a new beginning. When the woman who knew many men washed Jesus' feet with her sorrowful tears, He lifted her head and looked into her eyes and told her, "No more sinning. No more messing around." He then encouraged her and said simply, "Go!" When He said this, He was telling her to walk into her new life as a free woman, forgiven and clean."

> The world will see no value in your garden if you swing the gates open carelessly."

"Isaiah 14 tells the story of an angel who was once close to God but grew jealous of God and decided to exalt himself above God. But when Satan exalted himself, God saw fit to bring him down from his position of high stature to the lowest place possible. The Word of God teaches us that Satan has the ability to transform himself into an angel of light. It's no wonder that those who follow him have the ability to do the same. Maybe the handsome stranger with the sparkling eyes and voice of an angel can preach down fire and brimstone with the way he can quote scripture. But it doesn't mean that he is a child of God, and it doesn't confirm that he is the one God has intended for you."

"It doesn't matter that your friends are in dating relationships or getting married. God's timing for you exceeds that of current events or dates on a calendar or even years lived. His ultimate plan for you is perfect and needs time to cultivate. So, don't rush it. You can't live your life as other girls do. As a daughter of a King, your standard is a high one."

> His ultimate plan for you is perfect and needs time to cultivate.

"When you are tempted, ask yourself some difficult questions: What are my motives for engaging in this pursuit? What are his motives? How am I feeling emotionally right now? Am I lonely? Am I desperate? Have I sought God for the answer? God wants you for Himself, not to keep you from having a social life, but to protect you from harm and preserve your precious gifts for the one who is most deserving, whether it be for the prince charming He will one day send your way or simply for Himself.

Value your virtue, girl. God does."

In Reflection:

1. Have you ever considered being single a gift? If not, why?

2. Whether you are single or married, who or what has your heart? If married, what role does God have in your relationship? If single, how do you see God and what is your relationship with Him like?

3. Why do you think celebrating singleness is important?

4. Have you ever been through a period of singleness? Did it draw you closer to Jesus or further away? If further away, why do you think that was the case?

5. Whether you are currently single or married, how can you encourage others who are single and may be struggling with it?

Chapter 10
Darling Design

*"Not until the child is weaned; then I will take him, that
he may appear before the Lord and remain there forever."*
1 Samuel 1:22

The most powerful woman in the world is my mommy! When I think about who I am, I cannot help but
thank my mother. Of course, all the glory is intended for God, but
my mom gets an honorable runner-up to the Creator of the world.
My mom has an amazing drive like Hannah. Her Hannah-like
qualities were not the same, but the principle could be compara-
ble. Unlike Hannah, Mommy did not ask for me. She had no plans
for children really, especially a girl. My mom did not have the
privilege of growing up with her mother. She never had the experience of sitting on her mother's lap as a teen to talk about boys,
bumps, and babies. Although she was fortunate to reunite with
my loving grandmother in her twenties, my mom never imagined
raising a daughter of her own.

When I was about four years old, my mom changed my
life forever. Although I consider my salvation age to be ten, I am
now in a doctrinal debate with my memory about my faith at age
four. It was Easter Sunday (I still have the photo), and my mom
gave me a purple Easter basket. I was a child full of excitement
for everything. I thought that cutting the grass with my dad was
an adventure like no other, so I was excited to just ride down the
street. You can imagine how I lit up when I saw all the candy in
that basket! YES! I thought I was RICH. As we sat at the table,
my mom opened the Bible and starting reading Psalm 23 aloud.
She sat in the chair while I leaned on her lap, attempting to listen
as I really wondered what she was talking about. We had a GOLD
MINE sitting right in front of us, and she decided to read!

My mom knew I had about fifty questions at that point,
so she just started to explain. She told me that I had to love God
first. He created the world; He created my mom, and therefore
I was cool with that. He deserved to be loved. But what I could
not understand was her telling me, "Cherelle, I mean you have
to love God more than you love me." Um … what? That was the
worst news I had ever received in my four years of living. I think
it was the saddest Easter ever. I don't even remember eating the
candy, but I did agree to her demand. "I will love God more than

I love you, Mommy." No questions asked. You may not agree, but I believe my mother, in her own way, had just introduced me to my Savior, Jesus Christ. It was her way of giving me, her four-year-old and only daughter, the autonomy over my faith in God. I remember that day as if it did not happen over twenty years ago. Thank you, Mom, for being as Hannah and giving me to the Lord that day.

I have been blessed in so many ways. When I was pregnant, expecting a baby girl, I could not help but think about my life as a young girl. I knew Chris and I were in for it! I was that child, yes, that one to ask a thousand questions. I would say, "Mommy, I have a question," and she would always respond, with her semi-sarcastic voice, "Yes, Darling." And I would proceed with my five-year-old theories of life.

As I sit and write, I am anxious to know what motherhood will be like for me once Chloe hits that tender age of five. I still have a thousand questions, but thanks to Google, I don't have to always bombard my mom. How in the world am I going to teach my daughter to love the Lord first, that it's her design to only share intimacy with her husband, and that she is the most beautiful creation of them all? In the world we live in, how do I teach her to make God-decisions and not just good ones? Yikes! I only have my anxious spells for a moment because when I think of my mom, I am sure she had just as many cares. It eases my mind to have been raised by a tall, stubborn lady who would never let me settle for less than my best! So, Mommy, in your words, I simply want to say, "Darling, I love you!"

In Reflection:

1. Do you find it hard to love God more than a person in your life? If so, why?

2. How might you change your perspective and see the reasoning behind Cherelle's mother's teaching?

3. What does the Bible say about loving God? What does it say about loving others? (You'll want to search the scriptures for this.)

4. What are some practical ways you can encourage others to love God first and be obedient to His ways?

5. How can you keep yourself encouraged and accountable to loving God first?

ABOUT THE AUTHOR

Cherelle Johnson M.S. Ed, affectionately known as Lady J., assists her husband on the Pastoral Team at Divine Unity Community Church (DUCC) where he serves as Lead Pastor and Founder. She is the Co-Founder and Managing Director of Business Development at Consulting for Change, L.L.C., working with start-up businesses and organizations to ensure positive sustainability and community enhancement. She is the Founder and Director of IronDresses, Inc., a Christ-centered organization committed to living in the strength of our femininity. IronDresses desires to equip and empower women by teaching virtues of feminine strength through hosting conferences, facilitating retreats, and tailored development workshops. Cherelle is a double alumna of James Madison University where she earned her Bachelor of Business Administration degree in Marketing, as well as her Master of Science of Education in HRD.

The dream is for IronDresses to become an influential brand and a lifestyle. Cherelle is committed to developing educational and empowerment programming for women in different life stages. The vision of IronDresses, Inc. is to see restored and empowered women of all ages living in the strength of their femininity. If you have further questions or would like to invite this author to speak for a woman's group, please feel free to email the IronDresses team: info@irondresses.com. Visit our website to learn more about how you can become active with IronDresses Inc.

www.irondresses.com